Advance Pr

"Buried deep in this cap

Texas male politics is a

introduced a simple but quite subversive idea into Texas education. In an entirely unpretentious manner, she describes her efforts to inject into the public debate transparency about the results each school district gets for their spending. And, apropos to the rest of her fascinating life story, she describes the need to privately fund the effort after she left office. She doesn't point out that no other state has shown the courage to have such public transparency."

—*Eric A. Hanushek*, PhD, Paul and Jean Hanna Senior Fellow,
Hoover Institution, Stanford University

"*Texas Tenacity* is a compelling, insightful, and funny book from a woman with the audacity to pursue lofty goals and the tenacity to achieve them. Susan Combs's relentless drive and determination are legendary, and her tireless efforts have made a difference in business, politics, and public service. Combs shares personal stories, keen observations, and practical advice peppered with her self-deprecating humor to drive home her conviction that women innately possess the tools to direct their own lives—and they must choose to use them."

—*Lori L. Taylor*, Director, Robert A. Mosbacher Institute for Trade,
Economics and Public Policy, Texas A&M University

"Susan Combs's *Texas Tenacity* is equal parts memoir, advice column, and political strategy road map. As a long, tall Texan, she shares both inspirational and cautionary tales where she deploys her Texas-sized humor to smooth and ruffle feathers as appropriate. Balancing her passion to drive societal change through her legislative work with her family business raising cattle, Combs walks through the lifelong challenge of creating a fulfilling and productive life that allows room for family, work, advocacy, and volunteerism. Her experiences and advice leave you wanting to do more."

—*Elissa Ellis Sangster, Executive Director, Forté Foundation*

"To say that *Texas Tenacity* had me after the first chapter would be a lie—it was within the first paragraph. I immediately identified with Ms. Combs and when I read, ' . . . the fact that I had to define my future. No one else could do it for me,' I sat back and thought about how far I've come. This is a story of strength, overcoming, and standing for your beliefs. Ms. Combs not only shares her story but also inspires her readers to have the faith and tenacity to define their future."

—*Lisabeth "LB" Thomas, President, Texas Women In Business*

"*Texas Tenacity* is the ultimate call to women to take control of their lives and go after what they want unabashedly. Susan Combs's memoir is moving, funny, personal, and refreshingly honest about the hard work it takes to balance your priorities and achieve your goals. It's a must-read for anyone in need of inspiration to go out and make their lives happen."

—*Teresa Taylor, Former CEO, Qwest, and author of* The Balance Myth: Rethinking Work–Life Success

"*Texas Tenacity* is a must-read for anyone whose inner voice ever says, 'I just know I can.' It's a trust in the universe you can't explain to anyone, whether it be society or your parents or a friend. Susan Combs has an unparalleled level of curiosity, and understands that you cannot teach someone to *want* to learn by doing—it is inherent. As a business owner, I always tell my senior team, 'Give me work ethic and character in new hires, and I will invest my time.' Reading Susan's book confirms that what you hold in your head and your heart should always prevail. Susan provides the inspiration, knowledge, guidance, and most importantly, the confidence to help spur on those who dare to dream big and to act upon that dream. This was a very special book from a very special person—sit back and enjoy the ride!"

—*Annie Liao Jones*, *Principal & CEO, Rock Candy Media*

"Susan, in this humorous, winding tale of life, love, politics, and even fashion, gives women everywhere a great path to follow. We all have challenges to overcome in life, but with a little humor and a lot of confidence and tenacity, we can all rise above them and find success. As women, we need to stick together and share our stories with each other in hopes that our story might just make the difference in someone else's."

—*Melinda Garvey*, *Publisher,* Austin Woman *magazine*

"This book is interesting, fun, informative, and will empower women to know ' . . . if they come to a closed door, they have to learn how to unlock it, or they have to find a new door, or they have to work around that door.' The perspective that Susan Combs puts forth should be read by all women."

—*Toni Anne Dashiell*, *Republican National Committeewoman for Texas*

"*Texas Tenacity* is a guide for growing the self-awareness needed to recognize your defining moments, and more importantly—to act upon them. Susan Combs is a valuable example of how women can embrace their uniqueness and channel it to find their true talents and calling. After reading *Texas Tenacity*, you will be one step closer to grasping the hand opportunity is holding out for you."

—**Stephanie Breedlove,** *Co-founder, Care.com, HomePay, and author of*
All In: How Women Entrepreneurs Can Think Bigger,
Build Sustainable Businesses, and Change the World

TEXAS

Tenacity

A CALL FOR WOMEN TO
DIRECT THEIR DESTINY

TEXAS
Tenacity

SUSAN COMBS

GREENLEAF
BOOK GROUP PRESS

This is a work of creative nonfiction. The events are portrayed to the best of the author's memory. While all the stories in this book are true, some names and identifying details have been changed to protect the privacy of the people involved.

This publication is designed to provide accurate and authoritative information in regard to the subject matter covered. It is sold with the understanding that the publisher and author are not engaged in rendering professional services. If expert assistance is required, the services of a competent professional should be sought.

Published by Greenleaf Book Group Press
Austin, Texas
www.gbgpress.com

Copyright ©2017 Susan Combs

Distributed by Greenleaf Book Group

For ordering information or special discounts for bulk purchases, please contact Greenleaf Book Group at PO Box 91869, Austin, TX 78709, 512.891.6100.

Design and composition by Greenleaf Book Group
Cover design by Greenleaf Book Group
Cover photo: Big Bend National Park © zrfphoto/iStock/Thinkstock;
Woman © anyaberkut/iStock/Thinkstock

Cataloging-in-Publication data is available.

Print ISBN: 978-1-62634-350-4

eBook ISBN: 978-1-62634-351-1

Part of the Tree Neutral® program, which offsets the number of trees consumed in the production and printing of this book by taking proactive steps, such as planting trees in direct proportion to the number of trees used: www.treeneutral.com

TreeNeutral

Printed in the United States of America on acid-free paper

16 17 18 19 20 21   10 9 8 7 6 5 4 3 2 1

First Edition

For my parents, who taught me to stand tall.

*Throw me to the wolves and
I'll return leading the pack.*

—Anonymous

Contents

Acknowledgments

I want to thank my wonderful husband, Joe Duran, and our three sons, who never let Mom get a big head and have brought so much joy; and Lisa Woods, Reggie Bashur, and Martin Hubert, three friends for various periods of my life, for their integrity, intelligence, and humor.

I Double-Dog Dare You

Thirty minutes of TV changed my life.

I owe it all to Bea Arthur in *Maude*. You may remember her if you're over forty. Google it if you haven't seen the show. Maude had a cynical cast to her face, a deep, raspy voice, and a take-no-prisoners attitude. She was a very strong, aggressive woman, and she dominated the screen. What Maude said about something, you could take to the bank. The show came on in the middle of the workweek. In this particular episode, Maude was waiting for an old classmate to show up in town many years after their high school graduation. Maude had been the star of her high school class, seemingly destined for great things. Maude, the invincible. Maude, the bright star in her particular firmament. But now, here she was in her late forties, fading in her appearance, beached in life, acerbic, and not the powerhouse she had thought she was going to be. Greatness had eluded her. The classmate, nicknamed Bunny (perhaps because of her teeth back in high school), showed up with a whole new persona, someone totally different from whom she had been.

The gorgeous actress Barbara Rush played Bunny—glamorous, successful, and with great teeth—transformed, and everything Maude was not. If memory serves, Bunny even arrived on her own plane. She ran her own company, and her life was so much of a contrast to Maude's that I was riveted to the TV. The expectations Maude had nourished had come to nothing. The expectations of Bunny, on the other hand, had been dismal; Maude was supposed to be the star. Yet life had taken an unexpected turn. Bunny had changed; Maude hadn't.

I was in my late twenties working in a boring job in New York City, with no goal or vision of what should come next in my life.

I realized that I was on the verge of becoming Maude. My parents had sacrificed to send me to an expensive school, and here I was, doing . . . what? Working in a job in the federal government where I was never going to do anything earthshaking.

Some of my goals were strictly my own, some guided by friends or external events, but in no case did I ever believe that because I was a woman, I wouldn't be able to achieve them—one way or another.

The TV show woke me to the fact that I had to define my future. No one else could do it for me. That thirty minutes made me determined I would avoid the Maude trajectory. The next morning, I telephoned the administrator of the Law School Admission Test and signed up to take the test, cramming over a two-week period before going up to Columbia University for the exam. I received a good score, and I was admitted to the University of Texas School of Law for the coming fall term.

Maude made me realize that I not only had the power to change the direction of my life, but that I *had* to do it. We have to will ourselves into our futures, even if at first, the future looks murky at best.

In my own case, I would never have imagined, at the age of twenty-one as a new college graduate, that I would go to law school; be a prosecutor; run for elected office multiple times statewide in Texas—and win; and also spend thirty years running a cattle operation during much of that same period. In the meantime, I married a wonderful man with whom I had three sons, now adults; wrote a romance novel, which caused consternation in some quarters; and learned a lot about people. Lessons I still apply.

Some of my goals were strictly my own, some guided by friends or external events, but in no case did I ever believe that because I was a woman, I wouldn't be able to achieve them—one way or another.

> *Other times I faced closed doors—not because of being a woman, however—and either had to kick them down or get another door to open.*

I just didn't think about it. I am still not sure why that is. My parents weren't intentionally or deliberately "pro-women" . . . they just wanted their two kids to be happy and succeed. My mother wasn't a feminist; my father, as a rancher, was more concerned with rain and cattle than with my being a leader in any particular area. But together they cultivated good instincts in me and laid down rules for life that seem still relevant.

Plain speaking was welcome in my world, as were humor, great stories about individuals, and a love of language. These habits and beliefs brought substantial success and fun and helped me conquer and overcome obstacles several times. Other times I faced closed doors—not because of being a woman, however—and either had to kick them down or get another door to open. All of it was energizing! I retired from elected office in 2015 and projected that my next year or so was going to be calm, serene, perhaps even boring.

A new *Maude*-type event occurred a year ago. In the spring of 2015, I was jolted into a fresh awareness that society's views on women had not materially advanced in many ways. What woke me up to this fact? I really wonder why I hadn't been noticing; perhaps because the obstacles I encountered were the result of what I was trying to do, not that I was a woman trying to do it. I suspect I was rather insular in that regard.

A recent Austin, Texas, city council election meant that there would soon be a majority of women on the council. By way of context, Austin is well known as a liberal and forward-thinking city, even if not everyone agrees with its path at a particular time.

A male city staff member thought that this electoral shift was so significant that special training needed to be conducted to deal with this remarkable occurrence. Women assuredly were different, weren't they? Needed special handling? Presumably their brains were different, since their bodies certainly were. And yet there had been female council members before. What had changed? To this day, no one can pinpoint a reason why this happened, but it is noteworthy.

The male staff member hired a super special consultant team to deal with this earthshaking event, for who knew what might happen if staff weren't trained to deal with women! The result was probably not what he wanted or had imagined by the end of the consultant's contract.

Here's why.

The male consultant began by describing his experience base for how women learn, lead, communicate, and deal with issues—as a means of demonstrating his expertise and showing how he could provide help. Are you ready? He told the city staff that women don't like numbers, and they also ask a lot of questions. Interesting. As proof of these unassailable "facts" about women, he offered an illustration of the source of his experience and knowledge. Ready? He had been driving his eleven-year-old daughter to school recently, and in the ten minutes or so of the drive, she asked a whole bunch of questions— which he "answered patiently." Really?

Two things horrified me about this scenario and his words and assumptions. First, he used an eleven-year-old girl as an example for the best way to deal with adult women who are elected officials, who had run hard for their positions, and who had persuaded a majority of voters that they were skilled and competent. But second, he prided himself on his ability to answer "patiently" the questions from his daughter—his female child, to belabor the point—as if he were sacrificing himself in offering this remarkable service. On so many fronts, it was both a sad and frustrating commentary. It was also insulting and seemed to reinforce the stereotypes that are often repeated about women.

By implication, the male city council members accept and believe everything the staff tells them, never question any fact or conclusion, and vote in lockstep. Nice compliment for them, too! This all resulted in an uptick in national interest in Austin, with Conan O'Brien and a host of others commenting about the situation on TV. Not really what you want to be known for—either as a consultant or a forward-thinking city.

But perhaps the most striking thing to me was that this took place in 2015, in Austin, not exactly a bastion of conservatism. The social media lit up with people asking, "How on earth did the staff member, who hired the consultant, ever think this was appropriate?" I believe he is still employed by the city.

I have to tell you it got me pretty fired up. Nothing about the entire episode could pass muster on any account—not for women, or for men, or the assumptions and stereotypes that it perpetuated.

I asked myself a few questions: "If this could happen in Austin, Texas, how pervasive is this? Why is this view of women still so prevalent? Why were we even in this situation in 2015—and what do we do about it?" This last point made me decide to do something.

We did some focus groups on the topic of how women perceive themselves, and several things came out of that effort. First, the majority of the women expressed that they lacked self-confidence in the workplace. They didn't feel comfortable asking for a raise. They weren't sure they were ready for the next level in their career. However, they felt talking to other women was energizing, and they all enjoyed the sense of community they derived from speaking to each other. At a breakfast in Austin with about two hundred women in attendance, heads nodded all around the room as the three of us panelists talked about self-confidence. The word "confidence" spanned appearance, salary, life skills, future career, and the ability to get on or off the track they were on. It covered all areas of life. Except, interestingly, they all stated they felt most fulfilled in their home lives. Whether they had children or were single and childless, and happy that way, by and large felt they were "okay."

A recent lawsuit in the high-tech sector that garnered a lot of attention concerned the case of whether or not a particular woman was held back by her gender. The court found that she had been supported by males and that it was probably not her gender that slowed her upward progress. This lawsuit is an outlier as such lawsuits are pretty rare. From my observation, women are reluctant to rock any kind of boat, and a lawsuit is a very big, difficult vessel to manage. What also has cropped up over and over, whether in large meetings or one-on-one conversations, is that women repeatedly state that they don't feel women encourage and support each other.

And the perception of those of us who have achieved some level of success is that the women coming behind us are not at all as far along in terms of achievements as we would have imagined they would be by now. I absolutely would have expected 2016 would have seen full career equality if I had thought about it in the mid to late seventies. That has to change. So now, in 2016, I am embarking on a definite and deliberate mission: a mission to help women. This mission is taking two forms.

> *Being pissed off is who I am and*
> *I embrace it—and use it for good.*

First, I decided to write *Texas Tenacity* to show how women can have rich and varied lives if they recognize opportunity when it knocks. And if they come to a closed door, they have to learn how to unlock it, or they have to find a new door, or they have to work around that door. Or they just have to plain kick it down. Basically, we women have the tools necessary—if we choose to use them.

Second, we are launching a new website and social media effort called Herdacity, whose tagline is "Where Women Dare." Maybe this strikes a chord with you, or maybe you'll ask, "Dare what?" In part, it's for you to decide, based on where you are in life or where you want to go. Maybe you dare to be who you want to be. Dare to take a leap. Dare to express your opinions. Dare to change jobs. Dare to pursue your dreams. Dare to embrace who you are. Defining the daring is up to you, since each of us is different and unique. What we have is the unifying female gender bonding us to one another. We have a lot of work to do with the project, with its goal to educate and empower women across this country. I am really excited about it and look forward to seeing what we can accomplish—and how women choose to use these resources to dare a bit more.

Since you may not know me, let me return to my comment about being fired up. I had a wonderful business partner in the cattle business for over a decade, and one day he remarked idly that I was very "even-tempered." I mentally preened over what I thought was an accolade. With a deadpan expression, he then added, "Yes, you are always pissed off."

So there you have it. Being pissed off is who I am and I embrace it—and use it for good. It is also what prompted this book and the larger Herdacity effort, as well as a few job choices, running for elective office, and speaking my mind—even when it was unpopular.

Yes, I have dared in life, taken risks, fought and conquered nearly debilitating fear, seized opportunities, and held optimism close. With my life's pursuits, I have mostly focused on making a difference. I was powered by a passion to make a change or to achieve a certain goal. This incudes a focus on protecting children, changing a few things in our government to make life better for the men and women in Texas, and now to help one specific group—women. Although this boldness is a thread that has run through most of my life, I didn't always know it was there, or even how best to use it. But there are certain pivotal moments along the way that illustrate this determination and strength—and I share them with you in the hope you create a similar story of success and satisfaction and stand up and be who you want to be.

I wasn't particularly introspective in my girlhood, being more concerned with how others saw me and how I could and should fit into a particular environment. But I now believe that women have to help other women with advice, encouragement, and nudges—nudges that say to women, "Be who *you* want to be." Not who others tell you to be or want you to be. Only then can the real you emerge.

The pivotal moments that changed my life won't be yours, but you will have your own. Encouragement goes a long way to moving us along life's path, and we have to dare to keep moving forward. I double-dog dare you to be the person you want to be!

CHAPTER 2

Our Own Unique Narrative

If asked who I am, I respond that I am a Texan, wife, mother, and sometimes gadfly. Being asked who we are is a useful thing for us to think about, because it is the start of our narrative—who we are, what is important to us, and how we define ourselves. And whether we like our story or not, we can always change it.

> *Opportunity holds out a hand and we all have*
> *to reach for it. Sometimes our grasp falls short*
> *and we have to get back up and reach again.*

"Texan" as a descriptor is how many of us in this state frequently refer to ourselves—and I always like to start my own story with this description.

Why? Texans are different, as probably most Americans would agree, and our differences may not please everyone. We have a large vision of our place (some would say it is misplaced, arrogant, or just wrong). But it definitely informs our personalities and our belief that opportunity is there, if you have the gumption to go after it. We view ourselves as seekers of opportunity.

Opportunity holds out a hand and we all have to reach for it. Sometimes our grasp falls short and we have to get back up and reach again. Other times, we just aren't ready, but we will be. In any event, the huge influx of people from across this nation coming to Texas in the last 150 years or more is a testament to the power of this positive pull. We came here, and are still coming here, because we want to be here.

My great-grandfather arrived in Texas in 1854 from Missouri and took herds of cattle up the trail to the market for a number of years after the Civil War. He later became involved in ranching out in the area of Texas called Big Bend—an area known for vast skies, blue and green horizons, and mountains jutting into the sky. Big Bend's extremely dark, star-filled skies explain why the McDonald Observatory, some fifty miles away in the mountains of Fort Davis, has been so successful. His name was David St. Clair Combs, and he came with his parents and siblings, seeking opportunity that was said to be in abundance in this new state. According to family lore, St. Clair was not a family name, but taken from a much beloved family friend.

They first lived in San Marcos, a town northeast of San Antonio and southwest of Austin. He was of the right age to fight in the Civil War and he fought on the side of the South, as a member of Terry's Texas Rangers. After the war, he was very fortunate to marry a woman who was truly his partner. As a young girl, I was told how important my great-grandmother, Eleanora, was to the fiscal health of her husband and children.

David and Eleanora had three children, two daughters and a son, and his "Combs nose" is alive and well today after having been filtered through his children and grandchildren. My own has been watered down by my mother's side, but it has had a strong appearance in many of the Combs men. The first David S. Combs was also reasonably tall for the time, and standing tall has been carried down through several generations. (Did I mention that I stand at 6'2 1/2" tall?)

It was not uncommon for couples connected to the land to have to find a steadier income stream than what they got from the land, the cattle, or from farming. My great-grandmother earned a living teaching young girls in San Marcos, while my great-grandfather made and lost money with cattle. She provided a stabilizing economic influence without which he would have struggled more than he did. She was a strong and valuable partner, and all her descendants learned this from an early age.

Moving herds of cattle from Texas to the Dakotas in the 1860s and '70s was a chancy proposition with snow, ice, and blizzards frequently decimating many herds. But many men who fought in the Civil War found it a useful profession. They were skilled with horses and used to hardships. It was a long, hard trail, with many hazards along the way, and often the economic success counted on at the end didn't materialize.

What I learned from hearing stories about these dangers from my father, as he recounted his family's history, was that hard work was a constant, hazards were to be expected, optimism was a necessity, and perseverance was essential. You couldn't quit.

Why did I mention optimism? Because I think for farmers and ranchers, it is a common trait—and for the rest of us in our individual lives, it translates into hope and opportunity. My father, even in the midst of blistering hot summers, could shrug, look at the sky, and say, "Well, tomorrow we're one day closer to rain." Only an inveterate optimist faced with the likelihood of another several weeks or even months of drought could say that.

Sometimes in the late summer afternoons at the ranch, when the air crackled with heat, an unexpected thunderhead would begin to build. We would scan the sky anxiously, looking for signs of darkening clouds, an anvil shape for a thunderstorm. If it rained, even off in the distance, we could smell the witch hazel odor of damp greasewood, or creosote bush. It is actually a pretty worthless plant, not good for much of anything other than this divine smell. So even though nothing liked to eat it, its fresh, just-rain-washed fragrance lifted the lowest spirits. If you leave pasture gates open, cows will drift toward the rain, their heads lifted toward the sky. They know where the next fresh green grass will be.

My father also said on more than one occasion, "A rain and a baby calf are always welcome." That is so true. Sure, we liked calves to be born within two-month windows, if possible, because they gained weight at the same rate and could be shipped in large, uniform-sized groups, but they were welcome whenever they showed up. They would grow and could be sold, and the cycle of the ranch—and our family's livelihood—would keep moving forward.

Evidently his optimism passed on to me through the gene pool, or I absorbed it some other way. Later in my life, he told me how very much he enjoyed the many mornings he drove the neighborhood carpool and me to school in the elementary grades. Apparently it was common for me to start the day saying, "Today is going to be a great day." Each and every morning without fail. He told me he loved the memory of the little girl sitting next to him on the slippery vinyl seats, stating that the day would be happy, as if she could make it so.

I suspect I absorbed that positive and cheery outlook from watching my father, day in, day out, keep moving forward, no matter what he faced. I have tried to maintain that optimism to this day, since besides being natural to me, it seems that it helps to believe you have a happy star to guide your footsteps. A few years ago I even adopted (not to everyone's listening pleasure, because of the immediate fatigue level) the adjective "perky" to illustrate my outward perspective. "Perky" could probably morph without much difficulty into "jerky," but that is at least a beef product.

My mother came to San Antonio from St. Louis with her parents, as she was ready to enter high school. Her mother stayed at home, while her father, David L. Keiser, worked in the railroad business. He was an accomplished engineer, a very witty gentleman, and rose to become the vice president of the Texas Mexican Railway. He and my grandmother met when she was in St. Louis studying piano. I was never given any more details, and their pairing seemed unlikely when I viewed them through the lens of childhood. But they had both been handsome young people.

My own parents met and married in San Antonio, where they lived until their deaths. While my father was a Texan through and through, my mother exhibited the traits of a Midwesterner—she had a kind of pragmatism and an ability to get things done. I seem to have inherited her energy and focus on projects—just ask anyone in my family or those with whom I have worked. I consider it a gift, as it has allowed me to accomplish much, both inside and outside the home.

My dad was tall, 6'2", fair-skinned, blue-eyed, prone to freckling, and, like his sister, had somewhat reddish hair. My mother was 5'11" with fair skin, brown eyes, and brown hair like her father, who was proud of his Dutch ancestry. My grandmother was of Irish descent, tall, slim, with blue eyes and light brown hair.

* * *

I inherited height from both parents and shot up like a weed, as the saying goes, and it had somewhat unfortunate consequences, at least in the clothing area. What that meant was that my mother decided I needed "special" clothes, because I was so much taller than other girls my age. Special meant handmade, which meant god-awful. A local alterations lady, very long-suffering, was selected as the seamstress. As an example of the kind of clothing that was selected, my mother, for incomprehensible reasons, picked a fabric with large polka dots for bathing suits that were made for me; one was enhanced with bright blue dots, the other with red. People probably screamed when they saw me coming. I have to believe that bathing suits for kids—even beanpole kids who were 5'6" or 5'7"—existed in some retail setting, but my mother decided I had to have my own made. Wearing the suits around kids of my own age was a nightmare.

I quickly learned to enjoy being ignored. Getting tall really quickly, with clothing from *el mundo bizarro,* was not a good way to fit in, unless there was an alternate universe of dots looking for a new planet. I certainly understood from the bathing suit episode that the best clothing was the clothing that looked just like everyone else's. Camouflage in clothing was what I needed to aim for, if I just knew what everyone's clothing looked like. Why didn't I have a better idea of average clothing? I was a very shy kid and wore shorts or jeans, and hand-me-down shirts. We didn't have much of a social life, and what ranch kids wore had no relation to what city kids did. I also didn't pay a lot of attention to clothes until I had bad ones. Interestingly, but not surprisingly, this is another part of my childhood that informed who I became as an adult. You probably have a few of these experiences yourself—hopefully not with polka dots! My mother's clothing choices for me for college were even less conventional, but I'll get to that in a bit.

Halloween as a kid also meant my mother picked out outfits or costumes that resembled no one else's. From somewhere she acquired a Dutch girl costume complete with honest-to-goodness wooden shoes, and a stiff lace cap with wings that stuck out on either side of my face. I was quite the beauty. How on earth she found clogs in my size I never learned, but they hurt like hell and left blisters. I was grateful that the only trick-or-treating we did was on just a couple of blocks near our home. Being strange on your own block isn't so bad, but when your area expands, it isn't good. I would have preferred those terrible little masks that had the squeaky tight bands that snapped you on the cheek if you were a tad reckless. Those didn't happen.

But the street we lived on in San Antonio did have redeeming qualities. It was on a dead-end street, and, by chance, lots of kids were packed into this one block. There was always someone to play with. I got the idea of having a lemonade stand when I was probably eight or nine. The problem was that my concept of market research was flawed. I hadn't accounted for the fact that very limited traffic equals no big revenue surge. The cash receipts were a bit thin, but I gamely sat outside in the shade, waiting for someone to come by, stop, give me a nickel, and get a paper cup of lemonade. I sold a few, but the lesson was not lost on me that our street was not a shopper's wonderland and for future ventures, I needed to do better research.

I certainly had space on the ranch to wander, but because we lived in town, we had to make do with a smaller play universe.

But that block was a kid's paradise. An old lady lived on one side of our home, and her lot was so big, it ran through from our street to the next. It was a great children's playground, and I was welcomed in by her grandchildren, who lived on the same street and were my playmates. I was able to climb over her stone fence and roam undisturbed around her super-sized yard.

That was real freedom. Sitting in a tree, in the hot summer, with the sounds of cicadas buzzing in my ears, and no need to be anyplace. In my childhood, we could leave the house early on a summer morning and not return for hours. A bell ringing or various other means from other houses called us home. We ran everywhere with bare feet in the summer when we weren't on the ranch—leaping, soaring, with virtually no restrictions on where we went. I shudder today to think of that kind of untrammeled freedom. I did let our three sons roam pretty much the same way, but it was also on a very protected street.

I had learned a good lesson from my own childhood that kids need space to roam.

My father, like his father and grandfather, went back and forth to the ranch from San Antonio. The highway had been completed shortly after I was born; and my father—for about fifty years—drove out to the ranch on a Monday, spent the week there, returned to spend the following week working at his office downtown, and then went back to the ranch the following week. It was about 350 miles each way, and he drove it year in, year out, every other week. My mother didn't want us living out at the ranch because she felt the schooling wasn't up to her educational standards. I think she was right, but it made for a somewhat disconnected feeling at home. My father would leave and I would wait for him to return. At the beginning of summer we were taken to the ranch—with vast skies, a different climate, and we breathed differently. And of course, the room to roam was wonderful. I could ride, shoot, drive, and not see anyone else. I saw vistas, mountains that dominated the landscape. Just the other day, visitors came to the ranch and were stunned at the view. A giant extinct volcano filled our gaze, leading the eye upward. The sky was always the limit. We were free. I loved being able to leave the noise of the city behind, smell the different plants, feel the wind in my face, and be part of something big. I also was so happy to be part of a long tradition: producing food, doing the same kind of things people had done all over the world for thousands of years.

*   *   *

My father was very much a man's man. He loved the ranch, loved being around horses and cattle, loved the sky, earth, water, and grass. He was very proud of his lineage—of the fact that he, his father, and his father before him earned their living entirely from the land. He was also proud of the fact that he produced essential food for men and women to eat and enjoy. It was a very linear existence. He worked, he produced, and others reaped the fruits of his experience and expertise. He dressed in a kind of uniform for his environment: khaki pants, boots, white shirt, hat. Spurs for the times he was going to be riding horses. The hats were always Stetsons, with sweat stains around the hatband. Straw for summer and felt for winter—always the same type. He wasn't a daring clotheshorse, but he took considerable risks with the ranch. He acquired new and innovative ways of moving water through earthworks and long water systems. He risked capital and bought more land, knowing the weight of the debt would be a burden. But he made the correct kind of bet at the right time.

My father also worked hard to make the ranch fun. My first steed was a burro named . . . Burro. He was like many donkeys—slow, obstinate, and definitely not a racing donkey. We plodded rather slowly around until I got my first horse, a zebra dun. I named him Dunny. You are probably realizing by now that creativity in naming pets was not my strong suit.

I loved it when my father and I rode across the ranch and he would point out its various features. Everything looked better from high up on a horse's back. Not only could you see farther, which was a definite advantage, but things looked different. Contours of the landscape became more evident; a windmill a half-mile away could be spotted above the greasewood. The mountains to the west of our ranch house looked nearer. He really enjoyed talking about the ranch as a living, ever-changing environment. And the phrases he used were vivid.

Fort Stockton was about sixty miles north of Marathon, the nearest town to the north of our ranch. While we usually came from San Antonio along Highway 90, and knew that route much better than coming from the north, Fort Stockton was the big town where we sometimes sold cattle.

I don't know where he got this saying from, but he said on more than one occasion about the expression on someone's face, "He looked off into the distance like a Fort Stockton dog." I remember pausing, fixing in my mind the image of Fort Stockton. The town is located in much flatter surroundings than Marathon, and I imagine it was his way of saying the area was less attractive. But to me, being able to see a long way in both the literal and figurative sense continues to be important. In any event, his use of language was both picturesque and memorable.

Or how about this one, describing how dark something was? I don't remember the context, but this was also a favorite: "It was as dark as the inside of an old cow."

Not a young cow, or any cow, but an old cow. It was probably the cadence that made the adjective "old" essential. It was certainly vivid. His use of words and his relish for the images took hold. I wanted to hear stories about people on the ranch, or from his childhood, and I could see them as he described them. He enjoyed wordplay, moving letters around in a person's name to create an unexpected and humorous result. The fact that he so thoroughly enjoyed telling stories had to have been the reason that both he and my mother, a tireless reader, encouraged me to use my imagination.

*　　*　　*

They gave me a puppet stage, made of rough wood, for our San Antonio house, complete with two puppets, Bill and Sal (I named them), who were dressed in western garb. I don't know if my father thought I would be better connected to the ranch if I had cowboy and cowgirl puppets, but I loved them. They were mine and, boy, could they talk.

I put on lots of shows, mostly for my own amusement, and some for an audience. Bill and Sal had lots of fights, but Sal was spunky and she more than held her own. In fact, it was noticeable that she was the same sized puppet as Bill and she was every bit his equal. While my father encouraged flights of imagination, he also encouraged acceptance of reality. His influence on my adult life has been significant, and in that respect, he provided a different kind of role model, which was very much about hard, yet practical, decisions.

*   *   *

During the last part of a very terrible drought, he leased the ranch to a neighbor for three years. I was just entering my teenage years. It was very odd to have him home as much as he was, but it was still wonderful. I knew there was no rain, no grass, and that he had to do something. When we worked together years later, he looked back at that time and said leasing was the smartest business decision he ever made. He had been hemorrhaging money, and the lease gave him a three-year period to see if the weather would turn around.

Even while he was out of the cattle business for that three-year period, he never got over his absorption with weather. The drought finally ended, and he was always so pleased that he had taken the extraordinary step that he did. I have never forgotten that lesson. He let go of something he loved in order to save it; he found ways to occupy his time; and his practical, steely resolve was etched into my memory.

Because we had so much time during those three years, we embarked on a family trip when I was thirteen. I expect that daily his internal barometer fluctuated a bit, but while you are cooped up in a car for weeks on end, you have to have fun. Right? We were all veterans of western TV shows, and I had somehow identified with one in particular—*Gunsmoke*. It was a classic old western. Marshal Dillon was the law, Miss Kitty ran the bar, Doc was the required medical curmudgeon, and Chester was the marshal's not-too-able sidekick.

I don't know how I got onto this, but I spent hours and hours, undoubtedly ad nauseam to my brother, David, imitating and creating whole scenes where I was Mr. Dillon, then Chester, and then another one of the cast members. I changed accents, and eventually I began to run away with the characters until I had them doing things that would definitely not have occurred on TV but that seemed to fit my peculiar sense of humor. The car was small enough that I couldn't easily have been tossed out, but it would not have surprised me if there had been a significant effort to curb my flailing imagination. No one tried, and so I went on, and on and on. It enlivened my boredom and I think was weirdly fascinating to my parents. My brother didn't seem amused.

*　*　*

My mother did a very clever thing to assure that I would love reading: She would not let me read before kindergarten. But she had these marvelously illustrated books with fabulous pictures for me. I looked at them and kept asking when I would be allowed to read. And when I finally was, she directed what I read. *The Princess and the Goblins* and *The Princess and Curdie* were books from the late 1800s and, along with *The Secret Garden* by Frances Hodgson Burnett, they were books from her own childhood. They were not modern in any sense . . . except for the roles the young girls played. And later I read the Nancy Drew series. In all of these books, the girl was facing difficult times, and she triumphed—sometimes by herself, and other times with help from others. But the females in these books had power. We weren't just puppets—or if we were, we pulled our own strings. What a great lesson to have as a young girl!

Expectations from parents, society, or other sources can be the invisible puppet master pulling strings. In my own case, there was no expectation that I would ever manage the ranch; no expectation that I would have a job for any reason other than to fill time between college and marriage; no expectation or even desire for me to achieve any particular success. And grades weren't that important either. The phrase "a gentleman's C" could have been applied to my parents' expectations of me: to get "a girl's B." Yet I excelled in school, spoke my mind, and learned I could achieve whatever I set my mind to accomplishing.

There were, of course, other real expectations. Politeness to one's elders, good manners, and not getting into fights. Respect for others was drummed into me. But so were the cardinal values of honesty, self-reliance, and sticking to your word. These last three values were of enormous importance in the world of ranching far from a major urban center. Honesty was the glue that kept relationships stable. Self-reliance was essential because frequently you were on your own, and you had to survive and make do. And making sure you kept your word, that your word was your bond (a phrase I heard countless times), was a key element of any business transaction—and it was based on a handshake. You had to be trusted to uphold your end of the bargain. These all helped me in the business world, in personal relationships, and in public life, as they formed a solid foundation for my behavior. It was all part of the larger "education" I needed in life to ensure my success.

*   *   *

While my parents had certain expectations related to behavior that I was to adhere to, there was one expectation from my childhood that I did exceed—involuntarily. My height. I am really tall, and standing tall was something I was told to do in a summer camp when I was just a kid. We got awards for good posture. As the daughter of two tall parents, I had been expected to be tall. But I was exceeding their expectations. As a result of that focus at camp on my posture and the position of my spine and head, I achieved an erect posture. But I learned something else much more powerful. Standing up straight was really a metaphor for standing your ground, standing up for things, and being ready to take a stand.

At fifteen, I was six feet tall. That isn't particularly important, except that in Texas we could get our driver's licenses at fifteen; and I needed to fill out a form to obtain the document. We had to be described on the license: eye and hair color, date of birth, and height and weight.

No way on earth was I going to be six feet on my first and proudly earned license. The police officer just nodded when I said that I wanted the height to be listed as 5'12". He filled it in that way. I, of course, had figured that very few people would ever convert those twelve inches to another foot. That driver's license description lasted until it had to be changed because, yep, you guessed, it, I had grown some more. Two inches of difference required a new license. I didn't think 5'14" would be permitted.

Ultimately, after another few years of good eating, combined with the genes of tall parents, I ended up being 6'2 1/2" at age twenty-two. Although occasionally a person might say I appeared to be nearer six three, I very gently disabused them of that notion. Six feet three was way taller than 6'2" and change. That would have been too tall, so I resisted the description.

That kind of height on a girl in the 1960s certainly made me distinctive and, as you can imagine, caused its own teenage problems. The boys were all shorter than I was, as their growth spurts came later than mine. I remember agonizing over my height, as the boys seemed to get shorter as I shot up. My mother and I didn't really talk about it, which in retrospect seems weird, given how tall she would have been for her generation.

*   *   *

I do not, to this day, know what my mother must have gone through being 5'11" in the 1930s, but it undoubtedly altered her view of my prospects. My parents' engagement picture shows a handsome couple standing in the driveway of my grandparents' home. They looked strong, confident, and well suited. She must have worried about how tall I would become, because she asked the pediatrician how tall I would likely grow. They had some kind of a measuring projection and they expected me to stop at about six feet. While I exceeded that physical projection, what about the non-physical?

And how were those projections, or expectations, expressed or conveyed?

It is clear that, for good or ill, our parents have a major influence on how we see ourselves, what our successes in life might be, and how we view ourselves—at least initially. The messages we get from parents are pretty indelible. The mother who tells her daughter, "You can absolutely do that" is a powerful advocate for her child. The mother who tells her daughter, "No, that isn't possible" throws up an equally powerful barrier. My mother's fears gave me a lot of strength to face my own fears later on. Her fears were pervasive and created barriers to her expanding herself. What was she afraid of? Pretty much everything. We were on a trip when I was fifteen years old, visiting an old historic sight with a walkway around the edge. I scampered around and thought nothing of it. I was as surefooted as a goat and probably just as graceful. My mother was terrified. I still remember her telling me how absolutely and deeply scared she was that I would fall to my death or at least to a really big pile of injuries.

Fathers, too, can be positive or negative forces. Both of my parents occasionally sent mixed messages, but the overwhelming majority of them were positive. My great-grandmother on my father's side had been an integral part of the family ranching business through her earnings, and on my mother's side, my grandmother was also a force to be reckoned with. Any lack of perceived ambition for me was more a product of my parents' time and circumstances, rather than any lack of support.

Strangely enough, my parents did not ask me to make good grades. Whether they didn't want to put pressure on me or felt it wasn't important, I never could assess. But I wanted to do well. I wanted them to demand more. I occasionally wondered if, because I was the girl, it didn't matter. We knew my brother was going away to a prep school and then on to a good college. So without waiting for them to raise the education bar, I requested money for an A, an A-minus, and a B-plus—at different levels of cash. That small incentive that I had created helped keep me focused on results. As it turned out, I received the most academic awards in my graduating class. For those, I thank two excellent teachers from my high school: one who taught me the rudiments of communication through writing, and one who taught me to be discerning about history. The lesson they didn't know they also provided was that they were smart women, and they cared about us as individuals. They were excellent role models and I am still grateful.

As we all do, I tried to fit in and also stand out,
which I succeeded at doing, at least in my own way.

Through all of this—ranch life, city life, private school, public school—my story began. It formed who I am, helped me control the things I wanted to control, and started the process of me creating who I am today—or at least who I was earlier in life. Some of the strength and determination I have came from my parents, both genetically and through how they raised me. Fortunate? Yes, unbelievably so. But even though my parents had few expectations of me, I developed expectations for myself, and drove myself to do, be, and create more. As we all do, I tried to fit in and also stand out, which I succeeded at doing, at least in my own way.

CHAPTER 3

Fitting In and Standing Out

Education comes in all shapes and sizes and from many directions. Education in the typical sense is what you get when you sit in a chair in a classroom somewhere, with an adult standing in the front of the room, imparting his or her knowledge and view of the world. Another type of education, however, comes from observation and experience and a lot of introspection.

My mother, in particular, worried about the standard kind of education. She worried so much that she kept switching me back and forth between two schools: McKinley Elementary, a public school within a couple of miles of our home in San Antonio, and Keystone, a private school. The two were only a few blocks apart but were very different. Public school was free, and private education was not. But even in this time frame, when the ranch was under a severe drought and sustaining big losses in income, my parents thought private education was the right place to spend their scarce resources.

McKinley was the public school for our area and had the classic playground—it actually had two, one for boys and one for girls—with jungle gyms, which today probably wouldn't meet school safety standards. We had so-called monkey bars and we climbed all over them, and swung back and forth, heads down. I had a boyfriend named John in the fourth grade. We would meet at the trashcan at the corner of the building, which was the demarcation between the two playgrounds.

He must have been charming, because I was certainly charmed. And he was just about my height, which may have explained his appeal. I knew that I could see eye to eye with him. Some years I had a good teacher; some years not so good. Mrs. Perry in the second grade was wonderful, and Mrs. Parrott in the fourth grade was a stern disciplinarian who kept us all in line. I liked them both.

Keystone, the private school, was very different—housed in an old building and run by two brothers. Pops was very overweight, sweated profusely, and chewed gum. Coach was viewed as the smart one. He was intense and wiry. Keystone was known as the school where weird educational things happened, and maybe the students there were weird as well. But Keystone employed two educational strategies that made my later life so much easier.

The first was the use of a tachistoscopic machine, which was handled by Pops. This machine would flash a series of numbers, up to eight digits, for a brief time on the screen. We were to pay close attention and then try to remember them in class. If anyone got all eight, that student would get a piece of gum. Pops would throw the piece of gum out into the air over our heads. Only one kid was ever rewarded for a full eight digits. I think the gum Pops tossed out was Fleer bubble gum, a really disgusting shade of pink with a strong, sweetish flavor. This disciplined approach to viewing made me more focused and certainly improved my reading speed. I am convinced that I not only learned to read fast but to really pay attention to everything on a page.

The second approach was teaching us typing starting in the third grade. The teacher played music to help us get a certain rhythm and speed. My favorite for increasing speed was "Stars and Stripes Forever." We pounded away. I won third place, typing a little over thirty words per minute. Learning typing early was a huge help in college, but I didn't type in high school. We wrote all of our exams in blue books, which was a real burden since my handwriting was and still is abysmal.

In any event, my mother dithered a bit, and so I switched back and forth between the two schools. As best as I can remember, I attended Keystone in the first grade, McKinley in the second, Keystone and McKinley both in the third, McKinley in the fourth, and back to Keystone for the fifth. I was worn out. I never felt at home. Finally, I guess my mother wore out as well, and so she sent me to St. Mary's Hall, an Episcopal girls-only school a few blocks away from the two schools I had attended for the first five grades.

When I started at the new school in sixth grade, I was required to wear a uniform. I had no prior experience with a uniform, since at Keystone and McKinley, I generally just wore whatever was handy and in my closet. I honestly have no recollection of anyone dressing better or prettier than anyone else at either school. But a uniform at the new school? No one had bothered to tell me how it was worn. My mother didn't know either.

The notion of uniforms conveyed to me the idea I should be neat and tidy—in other words, uniform—so I tucked my middy blouse into my blue skirt and walked up toward the school, where I was observed, naturally, by lots and lots of girls in uniform. Not one had their blouse tucked in. It took what seemed like an eternity for me to snap to the fact that I was completely and totally out of synch with everyone. The educational lesson I received that day, before the start of class, added to my delightful earlier fashion experience with the polka-dot bathing suits.

But the fitting in problem didn't evaporate once I had untucked my blouse. Unfortunately it continued for a while as I kept growing. Being different is totally not fun in middle school, as most of us figured out back then. And being super tall is one obviously distinguishing factor.

If you're tall, you can hardly be invisible. You literally stick out. So if there is a clothing faux pas, it is nearly impossible to hide.

Shortly after I arrived at St. Mary's Hall, I discovered the school library; and for the next few years, I haunted the place, checking out books and retreating to a covered area outside during lunch period to read in blessed peace. I read, probably, to avoid other students.

If you are at all alert, there is always a message or lesson of some sort that can be gleaned from everything, whether simple or complex.

I was still very shy. And the social education I was receiving wasn't always kind. Education comes through many avenues: books, people, teachers, pets, you name it. If you are at all alert, there is always a message or lesson of some sort that can be gleaned from everything, whether simple or complex. When I was twelve, a litter of puppies was born down the street in a big brushy area. One of the other children on the block and I wanted a puppy. We each got one, and a new kind of education began.

While we still owned a much older dog, life with a puppy brought an entirely different perspective. It was through raising this puppy that the concept of unquestioning and absolute loyalty was imprinted on me. Scamp was a mutt, or as I later labeled him, League of Nations. He was smart, loyal, and always ready to be my friend. He wasn't a dumb animal; he was a smart friend, through thick and through thin. And believe me, teenage years have plenty of thin. I also knew that I was ultimately responsible for him, and I had to show both love and kindness. He had to be fed and cared for, even if I'd had the equivalent of a bad hair day or whatever passes for a lousy moment in your life. His happiness was largely dependent on my behavior, and conversely, many times, he was the key to curing the blues of the teenage years. At the time I subscribed to the theory that a human year is equal to seven for a dog, so we were both fourteen at the same time when he had been with us for two years. He didn't have dates, however, because we had "fixed" him. Since I didn't either, we could be home alone. He and I got through high school together, with a pretty inactive social life, and seeing his happy dog grin when I came home from school would brighten the gloomiest day.

*   *   *

I was also learning other things, being educated, as it were, in my own family environment. And my maternal grandmother's idiosyncrasies provided quite an education. My parents occasionally left me with her and my grandfather overnight. I had always thought of my grandmother as very proper, quite straitlaced, with a faintly dusty kind of perfume that probably came from ancient sachets in her clothes drawers. She would give me instructions on how to behave, how the "first families" didn't do thus and so. No description was ever given of the first families, but I knew from her tone and face that I was expected to behave properly and somehow fit in with this mysterious group.

Sit straight, cross my legs at the ankle, fold my hands in my lap, speak only when spoken to, be well mannered. All good things for young girls at the time. She also insisted I learn something about opera, and so each year I would go with her and my mother to at least one opera matinée. I wore clothes that were handed down from my older cousin, Anne. She was really pretty and a lot shorter than I was, so the clothes didn't fit too well. I occasionally had a dress of my own, which was dark, long sleeved, and not very delightful. I also wore stockings and low heels. Going to the opera was actually a wonderful treat. It was imbued with a kind of moral superiority that made dressing up for it important. But opera wasn't the only kind of entertainment she liked, I discovered later.

One Friday evening, during a routine babysitting event, the glacial image of my grandmother was shattered forever when we saw a different kind of dressing up and social opera. Without saying anything, she tuned the TV to the San Antonio Wrestlathon. What is that, you ask? I had no clue either. Evidently, years ago there was an arena in downtown San Antonio where, on Friday nights, men would jump in the ring and wrestle. I have no idea of the frequency or the time period, but those events must have been a hot ticket, based on the frenzied atmosphere of the crowd jammed into the arena.

My staid, Indiana-born-and-bred grandmother was galvanized by the sight, and she began to cheer on these burly men. They had exotic names and costumes. Some had capes, which I think were made of satin. They took them off with care and attention as they handed them to an attendant.

But the star attractions were the few and rare women who wrestled. One was known as the Bald Angel. She had shaved her head to prevent her opponent, also female, from grabbing her hair. It was fascinating. Here were women competing in what was literally a no-holds-barred event, amid screams from the crowd, with the referee yelling and blowing his whistle as he loomed over the struggling bodies.

But even more fascinating was the grandmother who was revealed to have the soul of a predator. She leaned forward, stared at the TV, and made what appeared to be knowledgeable comments. The action was loud, you could almost see the sweat pouring off the participants, and the thuds of their bodies made for great drama. I had known she was well acquainted with the various plot lines of operas and the great composers, but this was 180 degrees of social decorum off that societal compass. It put her and her strictures about social mores in a whole new light. It made her both more interesting and less credible when she issued her decrees after that.

Years later I heard the wrestling action was all fake. Oh, surely not. I had believed these men and women were actually injured—grunts, groans, thuds, and all. But was my grandmother a fake? How could she be both of these diametrically opposed women, so different in taste and style? Would the so-called first families she used as a social measuring stick have been glued to those same wrestling shows on the TV? I suspected not. So how to separate the wheat from the chaff?

> *Do the expectations that others place*
> *on us create a sort of "personality costume"*
> *that we wear for our external image,*
> *while inwardly we are entirely different?*

Education, as I said earlier, is obtained in various venues and through various media. My eyes had been opened: My grandmother was not the woman I had thought she was. But isn't that often true of people in our lives?

Do the expectations that others place on us create a sort of "personality costume" that we wear for our external image, while inwardly we are entirely different? How flexible are we in accepting our inner "I" as compared to that external "I"? We have all sat staidly in some hushed room while our brains are buzzing with a myriad of thoughts and emotions. Who among us is completely the same person inwardly and outwardly? I certainly didn't become the maniacal class clown in high school without being quiet and somewhat reserved for years before. And how do we treat others who display a surprising new personality twist that is at odds with the image we had of that individual before? Do we condemn the new person, or do we accept her "new" trait as an additional facet of a multi-hued individual? I suspect that the societal pressures put on women mean that we are more likely to have conflicting and unexpected traits. I hope we are accepting of these new images. My grandmother certainly had multiple traits. I just hadn't seen them before.

There was indeed a second event that forever altered my view of this elderly woman, and this one still makes me laugh. Dentistry must have been a very limited art in the late 1800s, since my grandmother had a complete set of false upper teeth. My grandfather's uppers and lowers were fake as well. What was at first enormously embarrassing, and then the fodder of fable, was how she took care of her teeth in public.

The Menger Hotel in San Antonio is a famous old hotel filled with history. Teddy Roosevelt stayed there more than once, and Ulysses S. Grant and Dwight Eisenhower did too. Movie stars, singers, and writers strolled through its lobby. The Menger hosted many of the most significant personages of my grandparents' times.

The hotel had a nice restaurant and it was quite a treat to have lunch there. We often went there for lunch after attending services at our church, which was just a few blocks away. We would swing by and pick up our grandparents, dressed in our Sunday best. For a while, little baby alligators were kept in mesh-covered cages in the main lobby, which added a delicious bit of fear as we sidled by. Would they escape? Would we even know? My brother and I would always make a detour, just in case the wire mesh was not on tightly. Then we would be seated, scan the menu, and order. We were eating Sunday lunch one day, all dressed up and minding our manners. My grandmother had always been something of a stickler for convention—until the day she deviated from the normal behavior of the other luncheon guests.

I still remember the amazing sight of Grandmother taking her pinkish-red upper teeth out of her mouth, powdering them with Polident tooth powder obtained from her handbag, and then jamming them back in. The procedure was accompanied by a very audible clicking noise. I couldn't believe my eyes or ears!

During the times I stayed over at night while being babysat, I knew her teeth were around somewhere, but I hadn't seen the installation process until that lunch. It was quite a show and attracted a bit of attention from others in the dining room, which she ignored. The fact that one of my parents was eating red snapper that bore an unfortunate resemblance to her teeth only made the scene more bizarre. To this day, red snapper conjures up double images.

I tried to process who this woman was. On the outside, she was tall, slim, tastefully dressed, and owned a developed set of rules of conduct. She had accumulated nice, but not always comfortable, antiques. Her dining chairs had some kind of itchy cushions, which didn't go well with bare legs and shorts. Her wooden chairs, with carved backs, made leaning back uncomfortable. Avoiding the backs was a side benefit of erect posture. I think my grandmother attended the St. Louis Conservatory of Music and must have been a piano prodigy, based on the beautiful old Steinway piano and stacks of classical music scores in her living room. The contrast of this culturally sophisticated woman with the one who adored wrestling and thought nothing of taking out her teeth in public was a real puzzle. Who was the real person?

This mystery about my grandmother told me that we are all multi-faceted and present different images at different times. Much like kaleidoscopes. If you twist the dial in one direction, sometimes we are bright and funny with colors that are exciting. Twist another way, and we are dark and gloomy with hidden spots that we have to deal with. Twist a third way and we do outlandish things that aren't matched by the external, placid exteriors we may show to the world. My grandmother was a doozy, but it made her who she was and she embraced it—at least in front of people she trusted and who would not judge her. This revelation gave me permission to have the freedom to be who I was.

All of us have internal and external personas. They don't always mesh perfectly with each other. But we don't have to choose between them. We can adopt one style for one set of circumstances and a different style for another environment. But we must recognize that the disjunction can be jarring. In the case of my grandmother, I was hugely embarrassed by her behavior in public. She had abandoned her normal social camouflage. But was I embarrassed because of my age or because I wasn't comfortable with myself? For if she didn't care, why should I?

*　　*　　*

Our clothing, our external image, and our visible behavior all combine to form a metric we are judged by. Fear of being dressed unlike our peers or of being with someone who is different can start at any age. Think about the polka-dot suits my mother made me wear. (The bad news about my clothing gaffes in sixth grade is that I didn't learn from them, so I was able to repeat them when I went off to Vassar at the age of seventeen.)

I had always suspected that my mother's choice of clothing for me was not the norm, but when I arrived at Vassar, my suspicions were confirmed. My mother had desperately wanted me to attend her alma mater, so it was a foregone conclusion that if I got in, I was going. Going nearly two thousand miles away was unnerving, but it had seemed inevitable, given the fact that my mother had hung a map of the school on my bedroom wall when I was about eight. I was on my way to fulfilling her expectations. I very definitely did not want to stick out in any unfortunate way.

Naturally, clothes for my college experience were a topic of discussion in the months before my departure. Not a very fruitful discussion, however, as it turned out. I was graduating shortly from the private school where we all wore uniforms, so my mother had little awareness of what girls in public schools wore. She hauled me to her saleslady at the dress store where she shopped, and they outfitted me with the wardrobe of a mature woman—dresses in knit fabrics, with belts. I looked like an eighty-year-old with a teenager's face. These wonderful items were carefully packed in my trunk and suitcase for my trip to the East Coast. My brother and I drove east, and he dropped me off at my dorm, with my luggage on the sidewalk next to me, and then he sped off into the distance. I had been studying the map of the campus in my bedroom at home for years. I was assigned to Raymond dorm, located on the main quadrangle of the campus with three other dorms, mostly in a dark red brick. The inner quadrangle was crisscrossed by sidewalks and there were signs telling students not to walk on the grass. It was late August, and Poughkeepsie, New York, was not a cool place.

There was a small desk right inside the door, with a woman in a white uniform seated behind it. I later learned that she was called the White Angel. I eventually managed to get my suitcases and trunk upstairs to the fifth floor, where I had a single room. There was an elevator that could be used for luggage, but otherwise we all just climbed stairs. I didn't find that a problem at all, since my long legs made short work of the climb. The process of arriving at college was so unsettling—I knew no one there, my brother had left me at the front door of the dorm, and I was far from home—that I was simply grateful to be in my room with the door closed. I had specifically requested a single room, fearing I would never be able to find a compatible roommate. The fifth floor had obviously been an attic and my room was small, but I could see out over the rest of the campus and I liked that perch. The floor outside was a really icky kind of slick brown linoleum. A set of white-looking coils under the window next to the wall put out intermittent heat. I had never seen a radiator before. San Antonio didn't have a great need for heating, even in the winter.

I had seen enough pictures to know that Vassar would be a beautiful campus, with a wonderful library, music building, senior dorm that also housed administration, and numerous other buildings. It was also quiet, since it was outside the town and was buffered by trees and buildings. One other feature of the time was that the students of a particular dorm ate downstairs in that dorm's dining room. There was no central students' facility at the time.

I was about to find out that San Antonio girls clearly did not dress like East Coast girls. We were light years behind in some ways, and weirdly advanced in others, but my clothes weren't in the latter category. And when you are in a single room, you don't have anyone to ask about clothing etiquette. Unpacking my matronly clothes didn't provide me with any further insight.

I remember putting on a dress for the first or second evening meal, which we ate in the dorm dining room. I was painfully shy, and responded rapidly to whatever question was asked. I talked very fast back then. A couple of days later a girl who later became one of my best friends asked if I were French.

"Me, French?" I stared at her. "No. Why?"

She told me that my very strange clothes and unintelligible speech indicated a foreign connection, probably French. That did it. The first chance I got, I went off campus to get the most conformist clothes I could find. That meant knee socks, plaid skirts, sweaters that itched, and loafers. Well, not exactly loafers, because there was no store in the area that had shoes large enough for me. That would necessitate a trip into the big city, Manhattan.

In any event, when I returned home at Christmas, decked out in my new "normal" clothes, the reaction from female cousins was particularly biting. Along the lines of, "Who did I think I was?" Well, I knew for damn sure I wasn't French.

Conformity in clothing can provide a useful armor, and a type of uniform. Dressed like everyone else means you can be inconspicuous until you decide you don't want to be. You are judged and classified based on your clothing. Today, young girls are acutely aware of their bodies, clothes, and how they look in selfies. It has to be extraordinarily painful to be instantly visible through social media. Even without social media, I was different—no matter what I wore, since I was so tall. And once again—I was the tallest girl in my college class.

I had one other weird clothing misadventure at a mixer at Columbia shortly after the freshman year started. Rummaging in my closet looking for something to wear, I pulled out a green velvet skirt suit and a green satin blouse tied with a floppy bow. (My mother had also selected this outfit.) We descended from the Vassar bus, and within seconds of stepping onto the pavement, a short, red-haired male much shorter than I was approached me. He spoke to me but I didn't understand him.

What I thought he said was, "Are you from the Fascist Institute?"

I stared back. *What?* "No. Did you say Fascist Institute?" Surely these students knew this was a bus from Vassar.

He responded, "I said the Fashion Institute."

I had no earthly idea what the Fashion Institute was but knew I stood out, once again, because of my clothing and my height. This theme seemed to repeat itself at every stage of my life.

* * *

After a period of trial and error to find my academic footing during my first and second years, I ultimately decided to have a double major: religion and French. French was easy for me, since I had been studying and speaking it since I was twelve, even if not very fluently. (Plus, it appeared a few people already thought I was French!) I had a natural ear for languages at the time, so I also took Spanish, German, and Italian.

Religion was much more difficult than the foreign languages, which was part of its appeal. The great religious philosophers thought long and hard about their subject. It was fascinating and occasionally impenetrable. It was certainly not the subject my family expected me to study. My father was taken aback by both my choices. French was not on the "good" list. What on earth was I going to do with it? Or for that matter, with the other sketchy knowledge I had acquired of three other languages? I was about a mile wide and a quarter-inch deep in language fluency. And as for religion, he asked if I were becoming a missionary. The idea that I studied the subject because it was fascinating seemed foreign to him. Yet I do not remember any substantive conversations about the educational path I was to follow, until I informed my parents of my majors.

Those four years at Vassar taught me how to think,
how to persevere mentally, how to work at under-
standing something—even when at first something
seems unknowable. I changed "I can't" to "I will"
and learned that "I will" takes time and focus.

I withstood the criticism with the comment that I liked both fields, that the topics were interesting, challenging, and surely good for my brain. I really didn't think about the economic impact of majoring in these two areas, such as how on earth I was going to earn a living.

I had no idea. But I knew that I could and would. Those four years at Vassar taught me how to think, how to persevere mentally, how to work at understanding something—even when at first something seems unknowable. I changed "I can't" to "I will" and learned that "I will" takes time and focus.

Several things became clear to me. First, I realized I could learn pretty much anything if I just thought about the topic hard enough, worked to deconstruct each and every sentence I was reading, and attempted to see if I could pull a string of logic through the material to the end. Second, I had good discipline and focus, and the ability to stick to a task. Third, I knew how to type. I could always be a secretary. But beyond class learning, there was another kind. My freshman year was the first chance I had to really break out of the old Susan mold. The high school me had been the class clown who never appeared serious, and who was smart but kept that hidden. The adventure of going to Vassar however had set me apart. I am still so grateful that my parents sent me to Vassar, where I could start to become the person I wanted to be. And as it turned out, the sky was the limit.

*   *   *

At the end of my freshman year, I saw in a magazine an offer from Cessna Aircraft aimed at getting people interested in flying. For five dollars an instructor would take anyone up for thirty minutes. Some ranchers had planes, but we didn't. I begged my father to let me do it. I don't think my father had any particular desire to fly himself, but I persuaded him that five dollars was no big deal.

The appointed day arrived, and we went to the airport. I don't remember being scared. I thought it was going to be fun. Thirty minutes later I was totally hooked. My father, probably seeing in me the kid partner he could mold, agreed to let me start flying for real. I only had the summers, so I knew I had to get cracking.

I flew first thing in the morning, when the air, even in summer, was relatively cool, and when there were no thermals to cause the airplane to pitch. I learned in a Cessna 150, which in retrospect was like strapping on a large box with wings to my back. It was wonderful! I would fly for about an hour, then land and attend ground school. Ground school consisted of watching films, taking tests, and studying. Then—lunch with the guys at the flight school office. Then more ground school and finally more flying. After three weeks, Monday through Friday, I had my pilot's license, which included cross-country solo and landings.

Every time I flew, my mother was terrified that I wouldn't make it back. I had to call her each time I landed, which I thought was ridiculous. It was clear that she had never had any expectation of me trying anything like that. While my father didn't either, ranchers did use planes in many states and across the globe to get around. For many, it was the ideal mode of transportation. I just hadn't shown any particular interest before. But that ad seized my imagination and seemed to offer all kinds of new possibilities.

The sights you see from a small airplane are unlike those from a large one. You brush the edges of clouds, and you do the turning yourself.

I continued my training after my sophomore and junior years, earning my multi-engine, commercial, and instrument ratings. The sights you see from a small airplane are unlike those from a large one. You brush the edges of clouds, and you do the turning yourself. You pull the nose up and do chandelles and lazy eights. You develop a deep sense of pride at the smoothness and control the hours of practice bring. The chandelle has you starting in one direction, gaining altitude, and then slowly turning evenly until you are facing 180 degrees from where you started. Lazy eights make the airplane's nose go in a horizontal eight pattern. And of course, you practice stalling the airplane, with the nose high and the wheel pulled back to your chest. And with the power dropping and the nose going off to one side, you push in the wheel, deliberately dropping the nose before you level out.

A wonderful man named George Baker was my instructor over those summers. He was a terrific, calm instructor. Just right for me. But he didn't always know how to tell me something about a particular aircraft. Guess he got embarrassed. One day we got a free ride on a DC-3 twin-engine airplane, and I was pilot in command in the left-hand seat. We were flying along smoothly when I noticed a particular item I hadn't seen before.

Down on the floor, on the left side next to the seat, was a funnel-shaped object attached to a long tube. I picked it up and brought it up to my face thinking it was some kind of communication device. George grabbed it and pulled it away from my face.

"What is it?" I asked.

He paused. "A relief tube."

"What?"

He repeated, "Relief tube," and looked down. Hmm. Relief. From what? Oh . . . sure . . . a guy who is flying would most likely need to go to the bathroom. I flung the tube down smartly. That really is the trouble sometimes being with guys. They just have a hard time being direct. Maybe it's out of politeness? Something else? I would certainly have preferred it if he had immediately stopped me before I raised that thing to my face. But, oh well; I learned something. Anything that looks like a funnel attached to a tube or pipe is probably going to transmit liquids. All kinds of liquids. So watch out.

That five-dollar coupon taught me so much in a larger way about life: You have to look around you—360 degrees up, down, and at all angles. Hazards lurk everywhere and relentless focus and discipline are essential. I quit flying at about age thirty, mostly due to a shortage of funds. Law school and its expenses, with no business reason for flying, meant that I couldn't afford to keep it up. But I still remember the exhilaration of the lift as the wheels leave the ground. You are up! When you make a smooth, gentle touchdown, the wheels squeak in an unmistakable fashion and the nose drops to level as you move down the runway until you can turn off onto your taxiway. Those were wonderful days, and I am so grateful to my father not just for letting me do it, but also for encouraging me. I suspect his finances were easier than they had been some years earlier during the severe ten-year drought, but he made a conscious decision to make that particular investment in me. He risked the money on me; I mastered new skills and became more self-reliant. These two changes paid off.

The next two years were spent with further studies of languages, religion, history, and literature. I also spent the summers flying and going to the ranch with my father. It was an idyllic time. The East Coast felt so compressed, with one town nudging into the next, that I occasionally felt stifled. Being able to return to the wide-open spaces and skies was a wonderful break before I once again returned to the crowded area north of Manhattan.

And the future loomed. What was I going to do? I did not plan on living in San Antonio right after college, since I already knew the employment opportunities were limited. There had been no discussion of my ever running the ranch. I needed to plan. During the winter, I figured out that I had to improve my secretarial skills, mainly acquiring shorthand and improving my typing. I made plans with three other girls to go to a course in San Francisco. It was all set up. We were to go in late June just after my senior year.

*   *   *

Everything changed in April, when my mother died very unexpectedly while my brother and I were back at college. We had just returned from spring break with my parents. My father was out of state at a ranching convention. She caught pneumonia and died in her sleep at home, just as my brother and I were returning to our respective campuses. She was only fifty-three years old. She was not the only person to become gravely ill that week in San Antonio. Another woman, much younger, also died from pneumonia, and a male doctor barely survived in that same outbreak. Graduation two months later without her was very painful.

I had to follow rules, be respectful, and treat people fairly. These were extraordinarily good expectations for me, and I did my best to meet them.

I had called her every Sunday throughout my years away, and those telephone calls were bright spots in my life. She had fully prepared me for college—just not with the right clothes. She was very fair and open-minded. Perhaps she brought her tolerance from St. Louis in her early teens, and so had a different perspective than others in San Antonio. Whatever the reason, she never permitted any kind of slurs about any group (unless they were relatives, of course!). I absorbed from her the understanding that fair treatment of everyone was not just right; it was mandatory. I believe her background and worldview made life easier for me on the East Coast. In some ways, I was less of a stranger than I might otherwise have been.

Being a long way from home meant that I was going to get homesick, but having a solid background from two strong parents was a huge bulwark. I had to follow rules, be respectful, and treat people fairly. These were extraordinarily good expectations for me, and I did my best to meet them.

I had fulfilled her particular expectations by going to the school she loved, and then graduating; and yet the person to whom it meant the most wasn't there to see me achieve her dreams. I returned home to San Antonio for the following year to spend that time with my father. I wanted to be there, he needed me, and I have very fond memories of that year at home. Ultimately I needed a job, though, and prospects in San Antonio were dim. In those days, women were expected to teach, be nurses, or perhaps work in banking. There were few other opportunities in San Antonio. I didn't have any particular vision of what I wanted to do, but I wanted to spread my wings. So I returned to New York and embarked on the next stage. Who would have predicted it would be so surprising and empowering?

CHAPTER 4

Be Brave

Sometimes even the best education and the best manners don't come together at the right time. But even the times when we believe something is a mistake or we make a misstep, something else—usually much more wonderful—is waiting for us.

When I returned to the New York area after spending a year at home, I wasn't sure what career I would choose, but I needed a job right away.

I knew I had to go to interviews. I don't remember getting any advice on how to master the art of interviewing, and I had never been in an interview before arriving in Manhattan. The interview with the head of McCann-Erickson International in New York was my second interview. The first one at Pan Am Airlines, now a vanished air carrier, hadn't gone well.

A friend of mine had worked for an executive at Pan Am as his secretary and arranged for me to have an interview at the airline. The building straddled Park Avenue and seemed very glamorous to me. It was June and hot. I had been job-hunting for at least four days.

I wore the kind of suit I would have worn for lunch in a nice restaurant in San Antonio. I was sent downstairs to a department that was called "Traffic" and seemed to have something to do with media. The woman interviewing me looked me over rather sternly, in my bright green linen suit, and muttered something like, "You don't look like you could clean out a filing cabinet."

I responded that I had heaved
lanolin-laden sheep over fences after shearing
and I could handle a filing cabinet.

I looked too nice? What was I supposed to look like? I was in an office in midtown Manhattan in the Pan Am building, and I had figured that meant dressing up. I responded that I had heaved lanolin-laden sheep over fences after shearing and I could handle a filing cabinet. I thought that would provide proof that no kind of work was too hard. It definitely didn't go over well.

First of all, what is a lanolin-laden sheep? For those of you who have not stood in a pen where sheep are being shorn, natural lanolin is the bright yellow gooey substance found on the sheep's skin when the wool is taken off. It makes them slippery if you are trying to get them out of the shearing pen and into another pen just across the fence where the already shorn sheep are milling about. It's easier to drag a sheep to the next pen than to lift it over a fence, even a low one. Think of a greased pig (which is actually a very smart animal), and then try to move a greasy, not-quite-as-smart animal that is wriggling. It is not easy. We got rid of our last sheep when I was about fifteen or so. I always laugh when I see someone described as having a "sheepish" smile or expression. I guess in this case I was the sheep, since I was ushered out of the office without further ado.

I vowed to do better the next time. Since I had been accused of being too fancy to deal with a filing cabinet, I dressed down for the next interview. It was with the president of McCann-Erickson International, a global advertising agency. I was asked to sit down in his office, and I handed over my resume.

He asked me to tell him about myself. I didn't understand why I needed to say anything since I had worked hard on the resume. I just pointed at it and suggested he could learn everything by reading it. He seemed slightly taken aback and asked me to tell him about myself anyway. So I did. I have no idea what I said, but I got the job and worked as his executive secretary for two years.

Early on I discovered that people from outside New York were viewed as being provincial. My boss seemed shocked that I didn't know a lot about Abercrombie & Fitch and where it was. But he was ignorant as well. I could tell any whopper about San Antonio and he believed it. Yes, of course we rode horses to school and the hay wagon showed up to bring hay for the supposedly omnipresent horses. Tumbleweeds blowing across the streets in our neighborhood—all the time? Hardly. San Antonio had over a quarter-million people, we had most of our teeth and fingers on any given day, and generally our family trees had plenty of branches. So there was some provincialism in New York as well. To this day, I am amazed at the misperceptions the two coasts frequently demonstrate about "flyover country."

My own horizons did expand in New York, and for that I have to thank the international and global reach of the agency. We were everywhere, in all kinds of places, in cities with exotic names, with interesting and diverse people from across the world. We had sixty-six offices in forty-four countries. I was able to remember phone numbers and names easily, and this helped me in my job. Unfortunately, my facility for languages also meant that I would occasionally and unconsciously mimic the accents of the callers in those far-flung offices. I particularly remember talking to a very nice gentleman from the Lima office. For some reason I began to adopt a slight Spanish intonation, realized it in my horror, then slipped into a weird British accent trying to correct the wrong accent with yet another. Finally, I got back to plain TV English. Sometimes an ear for languages is a bad thing.

About a year into the job, it became clear I needed a raise. I had accepted the first offer I had received and was barely making my monthly expenses. With respect to getting a raise, I decided to try a novel approach. My boss was the president of the company. His second in command was the executive vice president, the guy with control of finances and budget. I carefully wrote a letter, supposedly from my boss to the EVP, asking for a raise for me based on totally superior performance, dating back to the date of my arrival. I (the author) waxed eloquent about my talents, work ethic, and so forth, but it was so over the top, surely it would be obvious it was a hoax. I did a great imitation of my boss's signature (which I had mastered early), put the letter in an envelope, and handed it to the EVP's secretary (who happened to be my English roommate and co-conspirator) to give to her boss. Just in case, I left a copy of the signed letter on my boss's desk. Surely he would get the point.

A roar erupted from the EVP's office. "What the hell is going on!" A chair slammed back, footsteps approached, and loud noises ensued. The president and the EVP talked. A lot of raised voices, a bit of laughter, then silence.

Just ask for the raise. Be brave and
learn to advocate for yourself.

Did I get a raise? Eventually, but of course, only prospective, going forward, and certainly not backdated to my arrival. Lesson learned: Just ask for the raise. Be brave and learn to advocate for yourself. Less trouble and more straightforward, even if less fun. It also gives you that bit of confidence for the next time you face a bump in your path. Another thing to remember is that you aren't being pushy or aggressive to want to better your place in life. You are valuing yourself. If you are objective and clear-eyed, you can give an honest picture of why you are ready to advance. You may need to learn some skills in how best to present who you are and why you should be valued, but we can help each other in that effort.

Working at the ad agency in the late sixties was a fantastic experience. Places I hadn't heard of became commonplace locations with fascinating cultures. Think *Mad Men*. Men were the account executives and bigwigs. Women were sometimes creative heads, but always the support staff. And an individual female support staff was referred to as "my girl." "My girl will call so-and-so" or "do such and such." The fact that we could wreak havoc through sheer cunning wasn't lost on any of us. That letter didn't go out? Those copies weren't made? No guy knew how to dial his own phone long distance in those days, or could figure out how to send a telex (way before texting, faxes, emails), or make plane reservations, or call a cab. Nonetheless, I had a blast and it taught me a lot—about work and myself. I did any job without finding it beneath me. When you are prepared to do any task, you have learned something important.

My boss had made it clear that he expected my position to last for two years. He believed that smart young women would come into advertising, get a view of the world from there, and then move on to something else. The clock was ticking, and I only had six months of my two years left. What was I going to do next?

I was a whiz-bang typist and used my energy to get lots of work done in a short time. I put in long nights occasionally and came in on weekends in order to keep ahead of the paper blizzard. But I wasn't content with being merely the administrative staff. I was working so hard that when I finally left, I was replaced with two secretaries.

I was thinking about being a copywriter and asked my boss if he could do something. He said he would get in touch with someone in

Creative and see what they might need. I would still be doing my regular job, but he would arrange to get my foot in the door to see how I performed. I was very excited. Big breaks were ahead, or maybe just around the corner . . . but coming soon! From secretary to big business! I envisioned working on big accounts. General Motors. Maybe Tide. Perhaps Flair, a great pen company. Maybe a woman's hair product?

The folks in the creative end of the business were different—they created the ad and the image, but the account executives had to make the sale. They had to have the relationship with the client, deal with the pain if things went awry, and fix whatever went wrong. I learned a lot about sales, about people, about power games they play—and how to write. My boss was a great writer and he always sounded convincing. I think he genuinely liked every product he had to pitch, which certainly made his life much easier.

So, lo and behold, one day someone from Creative contacted me with the great news that I could work on a product! I could pick between Preparation H (medication for hemorrhoids) or Tampax (the well-known feminine hygiene product). Not General Motors. Not Coca-Cola. Not a product you can tell all your friends about. Hemorrhoids and menstrual cycles weren't the subject of cocktail party conversation, as far as I knew. It was clear, however, that there was not going to be any other offer. Take it or leave it.

No choice, obviously. As a woman, I had experience with one product but fortunately not the other, so it was Tampax. Was it going to be awkward? I had some notion it might be. Especially since one afternoon several months earlier I had walked into a male executive's office and saw, on the window ledge, two glasses full of water with several tampons in each. Guess they were there to detect water absorption—with real scientific rigor, no less. I did a quick about-face. The guys had no clue about Tampax. It seemed glasses in window ledges amounted to exhaustive research. So I sat down to write my first real ad for Tampax. To this day I don't know if offering me the choice of the two products was a subtle form of hazing—which didn't bother me in the slightest—or really all that was available. It was a challenge because I kept thinking of weirdly awful ads that couldn't be shown to anyone.

While I was trying to write bland and boring ads suitable for publication, I also wrote other ads—just for me. Puns have a way of rearing their ugly heads, and I won't repeat the kinds of ads I wrote then. I always threw them in the trash but enjoyed writing them anyway. Several of my regular Tampax ads did appear in national magazines, such as *Life* and *Look*, but I didn't tell anyone or point them out. Anyway, it was fun while it lasted, until I figured I needed to move on. The two years were just about over.

After those two years, I landed a job on Wall Street at a large company specializing in corporate finance and stocks. This was a complete switch of direction. During the interview, my future boss asked me why he should hire me. I told him that he would not find anyone with more energy than I had and that I would use it all for work. He was a very cosmopolitan individual, having connections in London and Greece. My job was to do routine financial analysis, spending time with red herrings and stock reports, and learning about corporate finance. Later, this experience became very useful. The majority of the personnel in the corporate finance department left, and we moved to another company. After about a year, my boss relocated to London. He asked if I wanted to go, but I preferred to remain in New York. I had a cat I was super fond of and I would have been required to put her in quarantine for months. So I stayed.

My next career step took me to a job with a federal agency, the General Services Administration. I had answered an ad in *The New*

York Times that said "large organization" seeks person with xyz experience. It was a very large organization indeed.

We handled all the federal property in the region, all archives, property management and disposal, and buildings. After about a year, I was promoted to work on the Federal Executive Board, which was comprised of the federal agencies in the region. We were supposed to achieve efficiencies through coordinating activities to reduce overlaps. It was a stellar notion but virtually impossible to implement. The very size of the bureaucracy, even then, was daunting. Paper in and paper out. Little did I know at the time that this would be a precursor to work I would take on once I became comptroller in Texas decades later. It was at this point that I really started considering what to do. I had already imagined what it would be like if someone lifted all of the papers from my desk and files, put them into a time capsule, buried it, and then opened it back up in twenty-five years. What would they think? Not much. Five years in New York had nearly passed.

*   *   *

In high school I'd had one date. Same with college. Girls' schools were not the best environment for finding romance. But I was also way taller than most everyone else. In 2016, there are many young women over six feet in height, but there weren't when I was in my twenties. New York didn't seem to be an easy environment in which to get married. My mother had told me more than once that, since I was really tall, I wasn't going to have as many choices. Sort of the notion that beggars can't be choosers. I remember feeling a dim resentment, but it was also obvious that the male population in my height category was relatively small. A glance around any room filled with a standard representative number of males would bear that out.

*I was twenty-five and thought I could never do any
better, so when he asked me to marry him, I agreed.*

While I was working for the feds, I met and dated a young man
from Estonia. He was handsome, had a great smile, and I thought the
cultural differences were exotic. He had lived in a displaced persons
camp for five years in Germany after his father was taken by the Rus-
sians and sent to Siberia. I was twenty-five and thought I could never
do any better, so when he asked me to marry him, I agreed. It wasn't
that I didn't love him. I did. I just wasn't madly in love with him.

Although I was married, the episode of *Maude* stuck with me, and
my husband and I began to talk about a new future. We agreed that if
we got accepted into graduate school in Texas, we would move. When
I was accepted into law school and he into a department connected to
psychology, we moved to Austin the summer before the start of school.

Then things began to go seriously wrong. I had known before our
marriage that he'd had some kind of mental breakdown in the past. He
told me that he had received a series of shock treatments to combat
some kind of fatigue and depression, but he didn't explain why. He
added that he was now fine. I had zero basis of reference on the topic.
In retrospect, I should have done some kind of research or done more
probing. Now we were in Texas, in a place that was strange to him.
Whether it was the dislocation of being in a new environment or other
events that caused a psychotic collapse, he became violent on a number of occasions. His erratic behavior didn't stop, and I didn't know
what to do. Somehow I guess I thought that being a tall, reasonably
strong woman would protect me, insulate me from harm. Nothing can
really prepare you for when someone you know turns into an unrecog-
nizable human who communicates only in shouts, fueled by an anger
that is completely irrational.

Years later the memory of these months made me
realize why abused women stay in relationships
when it is clear they are at huge risk.

I learned to fear his hair-trigger responses and reactions. I didn't even know what we could safely discuss. Yet, even with this situation, I did not confide to a single person that we were having trouble, serious trouble. I can't possibly describe how terrified I was. I couldn't understand the sheer irrationality and unpredictability of his explosive anger. What had happened? How could he be like this? Was there something I said or did to trigger it? I kept racking my brains but nothing surfaced. But I was still silent. I literally had no idea what to do, where to turn, how to cope. Years later the memory of these months made me realize why abused women stay in such relationships when it is clear they are at huge risk. We just don't want to believe he can't be fixed; we think it will all work out . . . somehow. And we are weirdly embarrassed. People will look at us strangely. What did we do? I at least assumed somehow that I deserved a lion's share of the blame. Don't ask me why I believed this, but I did.

A couple of weeks after one of these occasions, we went to the ranch at the invitation of my father, who was going to be out there for a few days—350 miles from San Antonio where my father lived, and 400 from Austin. It was then, and still is, very isolated. While my husband and I were driving in the house pasture, I said something that caused him to spiral out of control. To this day, I don't have any recollection of the immediate trigger. That was how it always was. There was a lot of screaming by both of us—his from rage, mine from terror. He was behind the wheel. I thought he might kill me; and I had no idea what had set him off. He stopped the car to yell at me and I jumped out, ready to walk back to the house, scared out of my wits. We were only about half a mile from the house, at a place where the ranch road was rocky and you had to slow down to make the turn. I thought I would be safe if I could just get out of the car, and he would cool down. I was on the side of the road, out of his way, but he aimed the car at me and stepped on the accelerator. He drove straight at me.

I thought he was going to run me down. Drive over me. Kill me. I jumped out of the way. I suppose he just meant to scare me, but it was so fast and so direct that I believe even now that he was insane, literally.

He stopped and ordered me to get back into the car. I was nearly stuttering with fear, but I got back in. I didn't believe I had any other choice. He could drive faster after me than I could run. We returned to the house.

I remember that night wondering what on earth I had done with my life. What was I going to do? How could I get out of this? My father and stepmother ate dinner with us and I didn't say anything. How I managed to get through dinner I have no clue. Surely I looked strained, or tense. But nothing out of the ordinary happened for the rest of the evening. Sleep was difficult. I honestly thought he would kill me, I just didn't know when. It occurred to me that I was going to have to defend myself in some fashion.

The ranch didn't feel safe because we were so isolated. I have read about people being next to individuals with weapons trained on them, not knowing when the trigger would be pulled. In a sense his complete unpredictability was a weapon. I didn't know when he would explode into a rage that seemed inexhaustible, I didn't know how to stop it, and I didn't know how to escape it.

Where could I turn for help? I kept hoping this was a temporary aberration. Even after the incident with the car, I said nothing to anyone. We left the next morning and headed back to San Antonio, then on to Austin. My father and stepmother remained on the ranch. I had not told them or anyone else of my terror.

I was about to risk making a
bigger mistake—hanging around waiting
for him to kill or seriously injure me.

Why on earth not? My reasoning was obviously deeply flawed, but I suspect it came from the fear of looking like I had made a mistake. I was about to risk making a bigger one—hanging around waiting for him to kill or seriously injure me.

Though we returned to San Antonio without incident, I still had no clear path for safety. I don't recall what set him off again, but around noon the next day, it happened again. All of a sudden he jerked me and threw me down the stairs of the front hall. He began to pound my head repeatedly against the stairs. I wasn't as strong as he was, and the back of my neck kept hitting the stairs. I thought I was probably going to end up with a broken neck—or dead.

I still don't know how I managed it, and can't remember if I hit him or just wriggled out, but I broke away from him, ran to the kitchen, grabbed the keys to my father's spare car, and ran from the house, barefoot. I was frantic. Would he come after me? Where could I go? I could hardly concentrate on what I needed to do, which was to find a safe haven. Getting the key into the ignition was nearly impossible because my hand was shaking so badly. I was afraid he would come into the garage and stand behind the car, blocking my escape. Thank God he didn't emerge from the house. I backed out, the car doors locked and the windows up, and roared off down the street. I kept looking in the rearview mirror. Would he come after me? Where was he? I didn't see him.

Through my fog, I managed to remember that a good friend lived with her parents just a few blocks away. I drove there and parked in front of her house. I knew I looked weird. How could I not? You didn't just show up at another person's house unexpectedly. You called, set it up. Even good friends did that. I got out and tried to figure out what I was going to say. I rang the doorbell. I was dressed in shorts, without shoes, and I imagine my expression was wild.

Fortunately, my friend herself let me in without hesitation after looking me over. When I told her I was in real trouble, she hustled me to her room upstairs. I told her what had happened. She had been at my wedding and knew my husband as a mild-mannered, smiling man. For her, it was shocking. This just didn't happen to people we knew. But she believed me, for which I am eternally grateful. I couldn't think of anyplace else to go. I don't know what she told her parents, but there were no questions asked. I was to stay at her house that night and to begin trying to contact my family.

This was a major crisis, and I knew—finally—that I needed help. I couldn't reach my father. It wasn't unusual that the ranch phone would be out of service, due to wind, rain, or something else that might bring a phone line down. I needed to call someone I thought I could trust, so I called my closest male cousin, who was also a lawyer. I told him that I had run away from my husband, because he had tried to kill me. I said it hadn't been the first time. His initial reaction was disbelief and he thought I had to be wrong. He said he had never seen my husband exhibit any signs of violence or rage, and it was clear he thought I was the one with the problem. When I finally finished describing what had been going on, the stairs, the ranch, the incidents in Austin, he finally agreed I had reason to run. Using the word "crazy" to describe someone isn't scientific, but I had no other explanation. My cousin put his legal skills to work and helped me figure out how to deal with the problem. Certainly a psychiatric evaluation and a brief period in a hospital were going to be the minimum for my husband. I am grateful that my cousin took charge of that part of it. I felt completely strung out.

After I finally reached my father on the ranch and told him what had happened, he confessed he wasn't surprised. I couldn't believe it. If he wasn't surprised, why hadn't he said something to protect me? Why hadn't he asked me if everything was all right? I remember feeling pretty much in a fog.

I had the dress, the invitations were out,
the reception all set. I didn't want to be the
one to break off the wedding. I didn't have the
courage to do it, and the thought of the
public ridicule at that time was daunting.

It was true that three days before our wedding two and a half years earlier, my father had taken me out to lunch and told me he that knew some things about my fiancé that made him think we shouldn't get married. He said he had done some investigating and discovered that my fiancé had been involved peripherally in a murder. According to him, the police on Long Island knew him because of the death of his best friend's wife.

But I had refused to believe my father. It seemed too made up. I asked him how long he had known, and he said he had known for months. I asked why he hadn't told me sooner; surely if it was that big a deal, he should have told me before we set the wedding date. He didn't have a response to that. I also thought maybe what he'd heard from the police was wrong—that he didn't believe them, either. Otherwise he surely wouldn't have let it go this far.

Then, as the final reason for me not to believe my father, I told him that it was just three days until the wedding! I had set expectations very high about the fact that I was getting married. He didn't say, "Don't worry, we can handle it." In many ways, his own conventional straitjacket had bound him as tightly as mine had bound me. I had the dress, the invitations were out, the reception was all set. I didn't want to be the one to break off the wedding. I didn't have the courage to do it anyway; the thought of the public ridicule at that time was daunting. My father was a strong man in many ways, but the notion of going against society's rules wasn't in his makeup.

Ultimately, my husband was picked up from my father's house in San Antonio by some kind of law enforcement (I was still out of the house) and taken to a nearby psychiatric hospital where he was diagnosed as a paranoid schizophrenic. I had to learn what that illness even was, what its manifestations were, and what kind of risks it was likely to present to friends and family. His earlier stays in a psychiatric hospital, which I hadn't really understood, began to make more sense. The marriage ended because I couldn't risk living with him again. What really added to my fear about him was the knowledge that I might resort to violence to save my own life. I began having nightmares in which one of us tried to kill the other. It was awful.

He left Texas and returned to New York after several months in the hospital. He was committed once again to a mental institution there, about six months later, after once again being diagnosed as a paranoid schizophrenic. I felt deeply sorry for him, but so glad that I was able to actually stay alive, get on with my life, and have a future. I had been a coward for nearly too long, and the adjective "brave" at first didn't seem to be a description of myself that I would want to claim in relation to other people. But we have to value ourselves enough to be bold, to take charge of our lives, no matter what seems to be societal barriers—which sadly, are usually self-imposed. What I also realized was that I had to reassess how I viewed people.

*   *   *

The messages women get about their men are frequently debilitating. "You can't do better." "You're lucky he will have you." "You are too [insert adjective], so this one is a keeper." On and on. The fear resulting from these messages is as powerful as the fear of physical harm and more difficult to eradicate.

You have to take control of your life.
You have to face your fear and save yourself.

How could I have been so wrong about the man I married? Questions that came to me in hindsight are ones I should have asked earlier. Revelations of over a dozen shock treatments should have prompted me to look more closely. But even without the psychosis, I knew other things were off-kilter and that those things didn't bode well for our marriage. One important clue that escaped me was that he had not been particularly nice to his mother. I just assumed that she was different and he was right to be dismissive. I now think the way a man treats his mother is one of the most telling indicators of how he will treat other women in his life—whether a wife, sister, or coworker. Respect for women needs to be deeply embedded.

Fear of social criticism led me to nearly making a catastrophic mistake. I failed in picking the right man. I failed by being too desperate to get married. I was more afraid of failure than I was of physical violence. But what did these failures teach me? And how many of us experience something similar to this in life? The failures taught me a lot. You have to take control of your life. You have to face your fear and save yourself. You can love someone but not be able to help him or her. I am still embarrassed that I let fear of social disapproval keep me in a very dangerous situation.

*   *   *

The way I had avoided dealing with the reality of my choice, the reality of what I was willing to put up with, became vitally important in the next phase of my life, when I was actually practicing law and dealing with abused and neglected children.

I learned I didn't have to settle for
second best. I was worthy of value. In essence,
I learned that I had to depend on myself,
and that ultimately I was my best guardian.

The failed interview at Pan Am and the awkward interview at McCann-Erickson resulted in me nonetheless having the opportunity to see the world in a bigger way and prepared me for a future in finance and the law. The exposure to the world of international advertising helped me shed some of the provincialism I undoubtedly had. And the failed marriage told me that I had to view myself—and those around me—more accurately.

I learned I didn't have to settle for second best. I was worthy of value. In essence, I learned that I had to depend on myself, and that ultimately I was my best guardian. One part of that understanding was that I had to quit using other people's views of who I was. I had to stand on my own two feet. Those lessons were hard learned but extraordinarily important. Women everywhere, of all ages, in all walks of life, need to be able to see themselves accurately—not through the eyes of someone else's expectations. And they need to be able to set out on a new course when life doesn't work out the way they hope.

I had no idea of the changes that lay ahead.

CHAPTER 5

Use What You Have Learned

I was nervous about starting law school, but so relieved I was safe. The semester started off with a whole new vocabulary of words for me to master. It was very intense. I studied each day—at school, at home, at night, and on weekends. Gradually the recent personal disaster receded somewhat and became less frightening. But it wasn't a subject I could discuss with anyone. Not a soul. It was still too raw, and I hadn't processed all of the myriad reasons why I had landed in that predicament. But I knew I had to. I would never, ever, repeat that experience.

I had started over again in a sense. The marriage had ended, and now the *Maude* lessons had to be utilized.

Law school was both a distraction and a welcome turn in my life. With its entirely different way of looking at events and words, law school was a revelation. Every word mattered. I knew from my studies at Vassar that words in literature, history, and philosophy all mattered. But here, how a word was interpreted might produce an entirely different outcome for an individual or a cause. The classes were tough, but fortunately there were a few women for companionship. We sought each other out, bonded, and the women's lounge in the law school was our informal living room.

I loved it. I know it must sound weird, but law school was a blast. I laughed hard that first year in my torts class. We all did. We had a pretty zany professor, Dave Roberts, who put an oblique spin on a lot of things, but we thought he was great. The first-year class entering that September was big enough that there were four sections, each about 120 students or so. Women made up only 17 percent, but we were a feisty crew. We were smart, not afraid of speaking up, and didn't defer to anyone. At twenty-eight, I was among the oldest in the class, and seven years out of college. I wasn't going to be browbeaten, and having recently been through a very personal, harrowing experience, I believed I could handle pretty much anyone. I was going to toughen up.

We had heard stories of the merciless grilling by Professor X or Y, which made us wince in anticipation. I tried to prepare for class as well as I could, but, just in case, I had a secret weapon. Callard & Bowser made fantastic butterscotch candies, which were so big in your mouth they would impede speech. When, during my first year, I was less than superbly prepared for a particular class, I would pop one of those great candies in my mouth. The giant candy lump in my cheek worked: The professor selected another victim.

I really enjoyed using my brain and absorbing the lessons from the cases. The weeks passed. The semester was almost over. We were within a couple of weeks of the end when another female law student told me she had a great brother—Joe—whom I ought to meet. Although my marriage had been legally over shortly after school started, I wasn't eager to jump back into a relationship. I wondered how she defined "great."

"Six-feet-four plus," she responded.

Pause. I slowly agreed that was also my definition of great.

We arranged to meet rather casually at the end-of-semester party at a fellow student's home. I wore jeans, and with high-heeled boots, was over 6'4" myself. He arrived; we were introduced. We started to chat. Somehow the subject became one we disagreed on, and Joe was so confounded by having an argument with a woman eye-to-eye that he pulled over a kitchen step stool, climbed up on it, and contin-ued the argument. That clearly set the path for future discussions—between two people with strong opinions who were nearly the same height. We have continued these same kinds of chats for years now; and it's part of what makes our marriage so strong.

He was the smartest person I had ever met, with the broadest array of interests, and he was completing his PhD in computer science. But I wanted to know how he treated his mother, which I knew would be a significant indicator of his views on women. I met his parents about six months after our first meeting, and it was clear he respected her enormously. His mother was very smart, with a terrific sense of humor, and Joe loved her a lot. He was the eldest of four children: two other brothers and a little sister. We married late the following year, and I know that for several years I judged him through the lens of my first marriage. I had to verify before I could fully trust.

Today, I will say that he is one of the most rational men I know. He digs deep into problems and decides only when he is certain. I, on the other hand, am pretty much an impulse purchaser. If I want to buy a coffeemaker, I spend about ten minutes on research. Joe, with his background in physics and computer science, may end up in a chat room learning about the vagaries of the particular models. But the care and attention he takes always pay off.

* * *

I continued to enjoy law school and got down to the books hard in my second year, earning the top grade in Business Associations and high grades in other classes. All of my grades went up and I had discipline and focus.

Joe and I moved to Dallas at the end of that year, since he had just received his doctorate and had accepted a teaching position. He and three other PhDs (one woman and two men) had started the Computer Science Department at the University of Texas at Dallas. They had the responsibility for starting a brand new department from scratch, and they were all working flat out. He had his plate full, taking on new courses, and also feeling the pressure to publish in order to get tenure. I needed to make a living, so I thought I would apply to law firms in the Dallas area. I was still going to school in Austin for that fall semester, staying with Joe's sister.

Graduation from law school loomed ahead in late spring, and the process of interviews was going to start. I hadn't worked in any law firms over the summers, working instead in the DA's office in Austin and then also for a defense attorney. Since law firms came to Austin to interview, I signed up for a couple of them. I had just learned I was pregnant at the start of the fall semester, with the baby due right about the time of final law school exams. Having had zero experience with infants, I calmly figured I could handle both a baby and a new job, right after graduation. Somehow, I kept forgetting the bar exam to be taken over that summer. My career plans during my fall semester had me believing that I wanted to work in a prestigious law firm and learn how to be a real corporate lawyer. And, of course, the money would be really good. Yes, a lot of hard work, but that didn't frighten me.

The first interview that fall was with two partners at one of those prestigious law firms. They came to Austin, where we signed up for a time slot. They held the interviews off campus. I had done some basic research for the law firm and learned that one of the partners had been a graduate of the University of Texas law school as well. I had been selected to be on the moot court team my second year, after winning a competition. So my name and those of the rest of the team members were posted on a hallway wall in the law school, along with those from previous years. I had put that team honor on my resume.

The younger of the two men interviewing for the firm mentioned that he also had been on a moot court team at UT. I was seized by an irresistible impulse of stupidity, so I asked him if he knew that for a small fee you could pay to have a pin light installed in the floor to focus on your name. (Had I learned anything from my New York experience?) He gave me a glacial stare. The other partner seemed to find it mildly funny. I received my rejection letter that same afternoon.

The second interview took place some days later at breakfast in a restaurant on the north side of Austin. It was a kind of big pancake-house type of place up on the interstate. The men were seated in a u-shaped booth with the applicant facing them. The sun came in through the windows behind them and right into my eyes. They asked me what kind of law practice I wanted, and I responded that I hoped to do trial work. "Why?" one of the guys wanted to know. I talked about the energy and excitement in trial work and then added that I couldn't imagine myself sitting in a back office somewhere dealing with dusty papers. Silence.

An interview is two-sided: Do they
want you and do you want them?

One of the men said, "That's exactly what I do." That rejection took a couple of days, but I knew as soon as I heard his response, I knew it was on its way.

Lesson? First, I really wasn't cut out for that kind of law practice. An interview is two-sided: Do they want you and do you want them? I didn't feel any camaraderie from either interview and decided I was the completely wrong type for that type of firm. Second, I needed a big dose of discipline and seriousness. Getting a job was serious, and surviving the interview was a necessary first step.

Knowing that I was pregnant and had just flubbed two interviews made me rethink my next steps. Joe and I needed to decide how soon I would go to work and what direction we would take. So once again, having a bad interview—or in this case, two bad interviews—set my feet on the right path. And the first steps were toward motherhood.

My first son, Alex, was born just two weeks after I finished law school. I had transferred to Southern Methodist University to finish a couple of classes in the spring semester, since I didn't want to be on the road commuting from Dallas to Austin and have the baby arrive early somewhere in between. SMU had a higher percentage of women in law school, but after the rough-and-tumble atmosphere of UT, it seemed to be somewhat stuffy. I soldiered on.

Unbelievably, I had actually planned to have a child born around that time! My reasoning seems like lunacy now. I knew I would have to take the bar exam, which required me to take a bar review course, which started in late June. Somehow I had figured that I would be ready to start cramming when a brand new baby was six weeks old. I didn't have any time to waste and a baby wasn't hard, was it?

I obviously knew zilch about the entire process. Yes, I bought books. But I was probably six-months pregnant when I asked Joe if our new baby would be potty trained at a year. He was incredulous. Where on earth I had gotten that idea, I had no clue, but it just popped into my brain.

I certainly learned that motherhood is much harder and more demanding than I had ever imagined. I wasn't prepared for the extraordinary rush of both love and fear I experienced with this baby.

We survived the bar review course, and the first six months; but I certainly learned that motherhood is much harder and more demanding than I had ever imagined. I wasn't prepared for the extraordinary rush of both love and fear I experienced with this baby. Why were his arms so much like spaghetti? Putting a long-sleeved outfit on him produced huge amounts of sweat—on me. I was terrified I was going to do something bad to his arm, since it just wouldn't go into the sleeve. He didn't seem to know how to do it himself at three weeks. *Gee*, couldn't he have helped a little bit?

Then he got colic. Pacing the floor was not fun. I was nursing him and Joe had figured out he couldn't do much to participate in the process. I had fooled him for a couple of weeks at first by suggesting that I needed to lie in bed while he went to the nursery and picked up Alex. Joe, being so intelligent, figured out I was either lying or uninformed—and being a liar seemed the safer bet.

The other thing I hadn't counted on or even contemplated was that I would turn into a giant mush ball. Joe, too. We would both sob at the drop of a hat if we heard music like "Amazing Grace," or saw something that made us think a child was going to be hurt. It was nearly instantaneous and clearly biological.

The other biological imperative that surfaced is that I would have killed anyone who threatened my child. Literally. I became super protective. Each breath, each whimper, produced a clenched stomach and fear he wasn't going to make it. He was my very wonderful little boy and he showed signs early on of being a whiz of a kid. He had my father's hair color (or what color he would have had if my father hadn't gone bald early), Joe's height, and a beautiful dimpled baby chin that showed up out of nowhere.

We survived somehow. His arms began to be more cooperative and dressing him got better. He smiled toothily and early—he had four teeth by four months and ate like a champ. He was curious and totally absorbed in the outside world. But as the months went by, it was time to put my law school training to work.

Joe was in the middle of his second year as an assistant professor in the Computer Science Department at UT Dallas. I figured I could now handle a job and a nearly nine-month-old baby. Looking back, I cannot believe how lucky I was to be able to spend that time with my newborn son. But it was time to go back to the world of interviews. A very good friend agreed to babysit Alex while I went downtown to interview. I had warned my friend I didn't know how long I would be gone.

Since I had failed so expertly at the law firm approach, I had been thinking hard about applying to become an assistant district attorney. How to start? I called the district attorney's office and received guidance. The hiring process was unusual, as the district attorney himself directly interviewed all applicants. Mr. Henry Wade, a famous prosecutor, was renowned for running a very disciplined, tough office. I was told to show up in Mr. Wade's outer office, fill out an application, and wait until he had time to see me. It might take two hours. It might take multiple trips. My recollection is that I had persuaded my friend to help me out on several occasions so I could make the trek downtown two or three times. I suspect showing perseverance, as much as any other kind of skill or intelligence, was a persuasive factor in getting me the job. For at least two of the times I showed up and waited, Mr. Wade didn't have time enough to see me.

On the third critical attempt, I had been there, in a chair, outside Mr. Wade's office, when I was called in. I approached the large desk with a view of the city of Dallas framed by the windows behind it, and noticed a brass spittoon on the floor by his chair. That seemed very fancy. Most men in my acquaintance just spit wherever, usually where a cow had recently walked. Just more of the brown stuff.

In any event, I was standing there and he asked me to sit down. I did. Nearly the first question he asked after he scanned my application was, "What does your father do?"

Not a question that could be asked today, but I answered because I figured he had a good reason for asking.

"He's a rancher."

He wrote something down on the paper and the interview progressed. At the end of the twenty minutes or so of the interview, I stood up to leave. As I leaned over to shake his hand, I looked down at my application, which was face up, but reversed away from me on the desk. He had written two words on the top of the paper: "Good applicant."

He had evidently decided that coming from a hard-working, old-fashioned ranching family was a good background for following and upholding the law. Plus, the discipline and focus I needed were there—and that made a difference. In addition, I suspect the fact that I kept returning indicated I had a definite focus on getting the job, and sufficient discipline to show up on time and be willing to wait. I was notified a couple of weeks later that I had a job in the juvenile division.

When I got the job as an assistant district attorney, I didn't know at the time what a major factor children and their lives were going to be in my future life. I didn't have any young cousins that I babysat or saw frequently, and the only real contact I had ever had was through the volunteer work I had done as a teenager at Santa Rosa Children's Hospital in San Antonio while in high school.

As I started my work in the juvenile division, the head of the office was careful to tell us about the two distinct types of cases we would be handling. Juvenile delinquents were handled under the Texas Code of Criminal Procedure and under the criminal laws in place at the time pertaining to juveniles. The child abuse and neglect cases were handled using the civil law statutes. At first, I thought I was going to enjoy the criminal cases more. I felt that right was right, and wrong was wrong. Gray wasn't a color I paid much attention to back then.

At least for juvenile cases, the preparation time was very different. The crime had already been done, and our job was to be sure our witnesses would show up, be credible, and stick to one story. I very much enjoyed it and was generally successful. One case in particular taught me a lot. A six-year-old boy had been sexually assaulted by a teenage boy living in the same area in east Dallas. We had two charges against the teenage juvenile: sexual assault and theft.

Even being able to get the six-year-old child to be permitted to testify in court was hard. We had to prove that he was able to distinguish between truth and falsity, which the judge had to assess. I had done research on the lowest ages for child witnesses, and my recollection is that six was pushing it. The teenage juvenile had been accused of sexual assault on little boys multiple times.

The day of the trial came. I was nervous. I had to be so careful not to coach the little boy at all, except to be sure he knew he was supposed to tell the truth. With the setup in the courtroom, the jury was to the boy's right as he sat in the witness box, with the judge to his near left. I was directly in front of him at the prosecutor's table. To my right and around to the left from the boy's perspective sat the defense attorney and the defendant.

I went through the usual questions to set up the incident, and then I asked the child to look around the courtroom and determine if he could see the person who had assaulted him. He looked earnestly at the faces of every member of the jury panel. I panicked. He was going to pick one of them. He kept looking at them. He even checked the judge out. Finally he said that he couldn't see him.

My heart was pounding. I was sweating. I didn't believe I could safely ask him to look again. At that time I didn't know what the problem was, but I couldn't risk an accusation that I was forcing the witness to identify the defendant.

My stomach hurt. The guy was going to get away with it. All I had left was a measly theft case, which was going to leave the teenager back out on the street, still a predator. The defense attorney then made the classic mistake—he asked a question when he didn't know the answer.

He asked the child, "Are you sure you don't see him anywhere in the courtroom?"

This was a new voice. Evidently the little boy hadn't seen the two people at the table to my right, somewhat out of sight due to the judge's bench jutting out slightly in front of the witness stand. He must have thought the voice was coming out of the walls. The defense attorney asked again and my heart was in my throat. I distinctly remember feeling my blood pressure rise and my heart beating quickly.

Finally the little boy leaned forward and he got a full view of the defendant and his attorney, and he pointed and called, "There he is."

I wanted to both yell and throw up at the same time. We had won at that point and the defense counsel must have felt like a complete jerk—he had asked the question that put his client directly in the victim's view, and the victim had identified him unmistakably. I had won, and a sexual predator, preying on little boys, would be off the street— at least for a while.

I have never forgotten that case and the lesson that I learned as a lawyer, which has some application to other areas. Don't ask a question if you don't know the answer, especially if the answer is really important. Find out what you need to know some other way, or don't ask, if you risk changing the outcome. I am sure the defense lawyer still remembers the case. Maybe he even thinks the right result prevailed.

* * *

While the criminal cases were challenging, they weren't as upsetting as the ones involving child abuse or neglect. The child abuse and neglect cases tore at my heart, and the images in the abuse case files were often so awful, so unbelievable, that it was hard to comprehend what an adult had done to a child.

There were lots of neglect cases, where the mother or parent in control was just indifferent or couldn't provide proper care for the child. Family members were often involved, but the help they gave was sometimes not a lot better than that of the mother. I say "mother" because there were few fathers, or stepfathers, or any male family member around. These cases had thick files where a caseworker would have documented years of trying to get the mother to take the child to the doctor, or not leave a toddler out in the street. Scarce resources at every level meant that continuous, long-term, low-level neglect persisted. There were always higher priority cases where children were at risk of further or greater injury.

In contrast to long-term neglect, the child abuse cases generally involved a specific act at a specific time and place. There was one case where a mother had been committed to a mental institution because she had killed her child. In the institution, a year or so later, she was impregnated by a fellow inmate. I don't know how they managed to find privacy, but it wasn't that unusual. As her pregnancy continued, the staff at the hospital became increasingly concerned. She made statements like, "I sure hope this baby doesn't cry like the last one," which suggested there was a potential risk to the new baby. She had killed her first child, she said, because it cried too much, which annoyed her.

In cases where injury was feared to a child, we could apply for an emergency court order without a formal court hearing. This was not a simple matter. Facts had to be laid out, then arguments marshaled and presented to the judge. In this particular case, we were able to get an order enabling the county to remove the baby immediately after its birth. We rotated these emergency requests among the prosecutors, and this time, I was handling the emergency order telling the judge that she had already killed one child because of its noise, and she was now talking about the coming child. Could he take that risk? We went back and forth on this, and at one point I was sure I was going to lose. I have no doubt that the mother would have killed the new infant as she had killed the earlier child.

> *There were and are lots of reasons*
> *we women don't protect ourselves or*
> *those close to us. We have to do better.*

That case has stayed with me a long time because the mother had done nothing directly to the as-yet unborn child, simply talked about it being born and perhaps crying a lot; but how do you assess the risk to the next child? The proverbial dog had bitten once. Does the dog—in this case, the mother—get a second bite?

Unfortunately there were a number of cases I handled where the woman had a boyfriend who targeted her child. I saw repeated instances where the mother failed to protect the child, and let the boyfriend cause serious harm. Often she was afraid of losing the boyfriend, of being hurt, and of not having an escape valve. There were and are lots of reasons we women don't protect ourselves or those close to us. We have to do better. I was once much like these women—afraid to stand up for myself. If these women had valued themselves, they would have been able to stand up for their children and themselves.

The photos in these abuse cases were always terrible. Joe asked me to quit bringing them home, or at least to quit showing them to him.

Our first son, Alex, was only nine months old when I started work downtown. Looking at him, thinking about how fragile he was, made me acutely aware of the risks to the kids we worked with.

One particular case was one of the primary reasons I paid attention to nutrition years after I left the DA's office. A woman gave birth to twins, a boy and a girl, and whatever psychological affliction she had before birth escalated post-partum. Our office became aware of these twins when someone reported them to be on the verge of starvation. They were four years old and weighed only sixteen pounds. My recollection is that the boy died and the girl survived. We knew that inadequate nourishment could have dire consequences, not just for physical growth but also for brain function. The mother had somehow thought they were perpetual infants, and she only bottle-fed them. Of course, they never received enough calories or protein to grow.

The child abuse cases became a passion for me. Whether it was that I was a mother, or that some part of me wanted to protect these little babies, these were the cases I preferred. If we did everything right, just absolutely right, we could maybe save a child.

*   *   *

Years later, as the Texas Agriculture Commissioner, I was struck by something that launched me onto a mission. It was the state of obesity in our children.

I had handled cases of children starving to death during those years in Dallas, and now, through failures to do what was best for our children—another kind of neglect—we were literally feeding them to death, sending them to an early grave from severe obesity. I heard from a prominent physician in Houston that this would be the first generation not to outlive its parents.

*I have seen some really bizarre foods in public schools
that were selected by principals and superintendents,
and I wouldn't allow any of them in my home.*

That gives me goose bumps still. How dare we not do what is best
for a child? How dare we take money from soft drink companies just
to have a football field sign or some other gadget we needed in our
schools? Much has been written over the years about the relationship
between soft drink companies and public schools—but the bottom
line? I believe it is wrong to put money before kids. Doing so is the
basic Mephistophelian contract.

But lest we be proposing a nanny state, we who urge better control
over children's food in schools are taken strongly to task. Yet virtually
every state requires, by law, that children attend school all day, for
many years, in what we presume is a relatively safe environment.

I think our obligation as adults is to provide an environment that
promises 360 degrees of safety: We have fences on playgrounds, we
have fire doors, and we have procedures so strangers can't enter our
schools. It defies logic to say that ignoring what we feed our (legally)
captive school children is not part and parcel of protecting them while
in the state's care, custody, and control. I have seen some really bizarre
foods in public schools that were selected by principals and superintendents, and I wouldn't allow any of them in my home.

Those years as an assistant district attorney also taught me that
there is a link between neglected and/or abused children and later
delinquency. When no one in their home or neighborhood cares about
them in a good way, children suffer. And society suffers with them.

Passion to help fuels advocacy, and that advocacy delivers the
result. When you feel the drive to help someone outside yourself, when
you are prepared to be relentless and persistent, you can accomplish

a great deal. I had to be ready to study, learn, and persuade a jury or a judge about a child. I had to be the best prepared I could ever imagine being. Everything hinged on me.

I lost only one case involving a child, and it was a case before a judge, not a jury. I later ran into the judge in Dallas. He didn't remember the case. I still do. The impact of what you do at every step of the process as you try to accomplish your goals requires you to be careful, marshal your arguments, find allies, and not give up.

Children, my own and others, have been and will continue to be a strong focus for me. I love my three sons, my three grandchildren, and every single day I count my blessings. I also make it a point to tell them that I love them. They say the same to me. It is a reminder that we are connected through love to those closest to us. And along my way, I was guided by someone else I loved greatly—my father—a man with flaws but many virtues as well.

Which brings me to another important lesson of my life. Sometimes things don't work out as we planned—but usually, often decades later, things become clearer, and we figure it out. So, decades later, I am still grateful I flunked the two interviews with the law firms, as those failures propelled me into an incredibly meaningful career of successful advocacy.

CHAPTER 6

Back to the Ranch

Sometimes those closest to us can provide the greatest guidance in life—and in such unexpected ways.

Joe and I soon had our second son, Blaise, in Dallas, and I returned to work at the district attorney's office after taking off time. I was torn between the work I loved and the demands of two children. I loved the job, but I also was beginning to think about my family's ranch and what would happen to it in the future. At this time, my father was over seventy. He had never indicated that he wanted or expected me to run the ranch, but I had made it clear how much I relished the work, loved the ranch, and thought it was a wonderful life.

I started talking to Joe about his future, his next steps, and I also talked about the ranch.

One day I asked if he would be wiling to leave Dallas and move to San Antonio.

"Why?" he wondered.

"Because if you could find a good job there, I could see if I could get into the ranching business with my father."

"What do you think is the likelihood of that?" he asked.

"I don't know, but all I can do is ask."

We talked a while about the cost of a move, whether he could find a position he liked, and what it would mean for my income. I was making a decent salary as a prosecutor, but by the time you deducted taxes, gasoline, clothes, childcare, and lunches, there wasn't much left. Maybe we would be as well off financially with the move.

I certainly thought from a parenting viewpoint that I would be much better off. I really didn't like leaving the boys each day and going to work, even though I enjoyed the work itself. The tug of war between career and family was intensifying, and I also really wanted the opportunity to ultimately run the ranch. I had seen my father's schedule and I thought it would be a good bridge between work and family. Joe thought about it and agreed. He had been to the ranch numerous times and was always eager to go back. While his childhood was spent largely in the forest and piney woods of East Texas, he quickly came to love the open skies, mountains, and high deserts of the Big Bend area. I called my father and started by asking how he would like it if Joe and I moved back to San Antonio.

"What would Joe do?" My father was definitely trying to be sure that Joe wanted to make the move.

"He is looking for a job in the area, and we really like San Antonio," I said, and then explained a bit about the opportunity Joe was looking at. We were pretty sure it would work out but needed to ascertain if my father really wanted us to come back.

I then asked, "Could I come and work with you and learn how to run the ranch?"

"Oh, yes!" he replied. I could tell he was genuinely thrilled. "I never wanted to pressure you, but this would make me so happy."

Over the nearly seven years we worked together, I heard both from him and from family members and friends how he had been so excited and happy that I wanted to learn about the ranch. I was absolutely ecstatic.

I know I solved a generational problem for him. Ranching was not my brother's cup of tea, but it most definitely was mine. I am so grateful that my mother had "educated" my father about how women think and how smart we were. In so many ways, she was a real role model. Although she didn't work outside the home, she was smart, funny, and took no guff. (I love those old words. Who on earth says guff nowadays?) If she took on a project, she finished it in record time and was nearly relentless about her focus and discipline. Yep, sounds a bit like me.

Although there are many successful women ranchers and cattle breeders, ranching is very much a man's world. My father and the cowboys were usually the ones on the cutting gates, where we sorted cattle for shipping or for working them. "Working cattle" covers a variety of activities. It can mean moving them from one pasture to another so they can ultimately make it into the pens. It can mean branding them. It can mean sorting them by gender, age, or condition. And you really are working. It was dusty, often hot, and lunch might be at 3:00 p.m. We had long days, because we wanted to get the entire herd of cattle sorted, weighed, on trucks, and headed to market by the end of each day. I helped in the pens, counting, moving the cattle along the alleys, and managing gates. I also kept the tallies so we had a good paper trail.

I loved my father for bringing me into
the authentic world of ranching.

Back then, the wives of the cowboys often took on the task of cooking for us during the '"works," when cattle were managed and sorted in the spring and fall. Keeping track of the cattle by group—that is, cows, bulls, heifer calves, and steer calves—was an integral part of the process. Sometimes the calves were categorized by age. Some buyers didn't want the small end of the calf crop; others wanted them because although the price per pound was usually higher, you often got a better gain starting from a lower weight. You had to keep track of all of the animals. The same was true with sheep. When we had sheep for a few years, the tallies were written up and down my arm with ballpoint pens. Thankfully, no one brought along a marker with indelible ink. I was taken from sheep group to sheep group and I remember it as huge fun. I was part of something that had been going on for thousands of years and it was very real. I loved my father for bringing me into the authentic world of ranching. Before the screwworm epidemic was basically eliminated, we dug worms out of cows' eyes. In the summer we helped brand cattle; worked sheep; ate late or not at all; rose early and showed up before daylight—on horseback or not, depending. I was one of the guys and it felt great. The entire rhythm and flow of that work was and still is fascinating.

The way my father and I arranged our partnership was simple. We shared a one-room office in the Milam Building in downtown San Antonio for seven years until he passed away unexpectedly. Two desks about six feet apart, some filing cabinets, a sofa, and a long table that caught a lot of overflow. It was a perfect setting for learning directly from him, and I was very happy to be an adult working with an adult parent. We weren't equals, but we were partners, with respect and admiration between us.

And I loved how he talked. We talked every day on a whole range of topics, and on the long drives to the ranch. He was very happy to have company, and I learned so much from riding around the ranch with him, taking notes, and listening. What a gift.

I was working in the ranch office and also in a law firm, and raising two, then three sons. The ranch location necessitated frequent absence from our home. I was very fortunate to have such a supportive husband who believes my happiness and pursuits are just as important as his own. Maybe this is more common today, but we married over forty years ago, and it was a bit anomalous for the time. But the fact that I recognize these endearing qualities about him doesn't stop me from giving him and our three sons an occasional bit of hell. That may be why our youngest son named me Evil Mom Lady some years back.

Because I was surrounded by men both at home and on the ranch, I insisted on always having female pets—cats and dogs. I never felt overwhelmed. Boys' laundry, clutter, smells—all were great.

Being in a man's world at home and at work, however, did require adjustments. Imagine you're out in far West Texas, with the occasional cactus, windmill, and tank. You have to go to the bathroom. And even worse, you're really tall. The cowboys are working in the pens and you just step out to take care of nature's call. First, you look for cover. Remember, this is the high desert; you've got low plants, low cactus, some scrubby greasewood, not really any trees. Then you realize you have to get behind the metal water tank, which is about five feet tall. Yes, it is shorter than your head so you have to accommodate. You do so successfully and rush back, hoping no one noticed your departure.

I realize this is probably TMI, but this kind of conundrum is real. Men and women traveling together have to deal with different natural processes. Who gets embarrassed? How can you avoid it? Being bold usually works.

Another thing I loved about my father was his very strong friendships with longtime friends, and the one he had with a longtime employee. This was a friendship that he cherished, but that also exasperated him. It was with Blas Payne, pronounced Bloss, like floss. Blas came to work on the ranch in 1919 at the age of eighteen and died in Alpine after a brief illness in 1989, two years after my father. Blas loved cows and he would sneak extra feed to them. My father thought of him as an exemplary cowman and also someone who would frustrate his spending goals. But when the Post Ranch calves, which Blas oversaw, came in heavier than elsewhere, my father would smile.

Blas evidently had a somewhat checkered past. He would go to Fort Stockton, which he called "Comanche" because of the Comanche Springs, and he would overindulge and be thrown into the local jail. My father would drive the seventy-plus miles north, get him out of jail, and bring him back to the ranch. Their friendship was enduring, with mutual respect between them.

> *I absolutely learned the value of loyalty,*
> *of long-term working relationships,*
> *and that loyalty runs both ways.*

I also held great admiration for Blas. He knew ranching, and he had an extraordinary dedication to the cattle. He also was a good ranch tutor to me. We spent a lot of time together over the years, and he helped me tremendously. Thinking back, there was only one time when Blas asked for something, and it was after my father died. He asked to be buried on the ranch. We selected a spot where he is today, up on a hill, and on the way to one of the big pastures. He also asked me to wave at him as I drove past, and I still do, more than twenty-five years later. He was a wonderful, smart, and unique individual. We were lucky to be able to work with him for so many years. From this, I absolutely learned the value of loyalty, of long-term working relationships, and that loyalty runs both ways. Our middle son, Blaise, was named both for Blas and for Blaise Pascal, the famous French mathematician and inventor from the 1600s.

When your chosen profession has you working and competing in a fairly tough physical environment, your ability to withstand those physical stresses counts. My father would speak admiringly of both men and women by saying, "He or she is as tough as an old boot." He meant an old boot that he wore for years, that fit, and that kept on working. An old boot was tough, but it was a friend. It withstood thorns, barbed wire, cow manure in the pens, and the occasional soaking when rare rains fell. I still have his old boots. He was as tough as an old boot, too.

On a particular occasion, my father demonstrated calm in the face of what otherwise might have seemed a social calamity. The Milam building, where we worked in San Antonio, had a café on the first floor and we often ate there for lunch—usually a hamburger. The small coffee shop and restaurant was on a corner of a busy downtown intersection. We did that with regularity for several years. My father had named it Club Linoleum. There were several rows of booths, and pretty dingy linoleum. One day something out of the ordinary happened.

A worker came running out from the kitchen, holding a broom high over his head. He ran down the center aisle past where we were seated in a booth on one side. What on earth was he doing? A small movement caught my eye. A mouse was fleeing the encroaching monster and running down the center aisle. Everyone sat back to observe the outcome. The mouse was dispatched efficiently. There was a brief respectful silence.

My father calmly picked up the rest of his hamburger and proceeded to finish it. No worries about health issues troubled him. I followed suit. We continued to eat there regularly and that was the last mouse we saw fleeing the kitchen. It later occurred to me that perhaps the mouse was escaping from the cuisine and not the broom, and was trying to issue a warning.

* * *

We stayed in San Antonio for five years, until the pull of Joe's new venture, a high-tech startup with two friends, took us back to Austin. I continued to drive to San Antonio each day, working closely with my father on the many parts of running our family's ranch.

Over the second Christmas holiday after our move to Austin, my father suffered a heart ailment. He had had several heart attacks years earlier. In January, he had a repair done that was considered extremely successful. He was released from the hospital and suffered a final, irreversible heart attack that same evening at home.

Of course, this was a huge shock, since he had been expected to make a full recovery and have many more years of healthy life.

To say it was hard to lose my father is an understatement. We hadn't spent much time together earlier in my life because of his trips to the ranch every other week, but working together in the same office in San Antonio for so many years later had been a gift. I knew I was going to miss him—and our conversations—tremendously. This was primarily because my father had stepped out of the parent role and had become my mentor over the past few years. Through his words I learned the practical ins and outs of running the ranch. But through his actions I learned the greatness of what it meant to be a fair, honest, and respected leader who made decisions quickly and carefully, who shared the "glory" of success with everyone involved, and who kept his word. It's not as if my father threw his weight around; but just by his sheer presence, people knew he was in charge, he had answers, and that everything would be okay. I realized how much I had grown over those seven years—and in so many ways. I was still the strong, smart, and determined person I was when I started, but I had greater depth, if you will. Those were lessons I carried with me, and they were invaluable.

I had essentially gotten off the career escalator that had been carrying me upward. I worried somewhat about what I would do next, and when.

His death also gave me the chance to refocus my priorities. The ranch was a legacy from my family going back over a hundred years. Now, as executor of the estate, I had to focus primarily on the legal affairs—along with running the ranch. I immediately quit the law firm where I was working part time, shut the San Antonio ranch office, and opened one with all of the appropriate ranch-related files in Austin. Our kids were in school in Austin, and Joe was anchored there as well. I realized that I was about to remake my day into something much better—a day where I did ranch-related work during school hours, and then devoted the rest of my time to the kids. Immediately my stress level plummeted, and so did the family's. I was able to have a rational daily schedule: office in the mornings, kids in the afternoon.

I had essentially gotten off the career escalator that had been carrying me upward. I worried somewhat about what I would do next, and when.

One area of life that continued was, of course, the ranch. I figured out that if I wanted to manage the ranch and spend time with my family, at a distance of four hundred miles, I needed eyes and ears closer at hand. And this individual had to be someone with skin in the game.

My father, intelligent as always, was thinking the same thing a few years earlier, and he established a working relationship with a fine rancher from Marfa, about sixty miles away. I thought a lot of Gene West. A few months after my father's death, I asked him if he would consider becoming a full partner, taking over my brother's half interest in the cattle and leasing his share of the ranch. He accepted and we had a very successful partnership for fifteen years until a major drought forced us to shut down our joint cattle operation in 2002.

I learned a lot from Gene. He, like my father, knew a great deal about cattle, and I could count on him to be a clear-eyed, savvy partner. My parents and his in-laws had been lifelong friends, so I already knew Gene and his family. The Trans-Pecos area of Texas is both large in scope and small in the way neighbors feel about each other—even at fifty- and one-hundred-mile gaps. His knowledge of cattle, water systems, and general ranching was invaluable. As I pointed out in the introduction, he had no problem in straight talking, since it was Gene who said I was "so even tempered—always pissed off." His exact words.

*　　*　　*

But I was still trying to figure out who and what I wanted to be in addition to running the ranch. It may be that my motor had revved at such a high speed for so long that I was finding it a bit hard to adjust to a slower pace. My children were gone every day, and I didn't want to take on any new volunteer tasks. What could I do? Was there anything in town that I could do during the day? I knew I couldn't try a new law firm since that would require a big time commitment. I needed to be able to pick up and go to the ranch whenever I needed to. Therefore, any other activities I took on had to allow flexibility.

So what next? And, more importantly, when? Every phase of life you are in is different from that before and after, and one of our essential skills as individuals is to be able to detect those changes as they occur, and to be ready to seize the opportunity when it appears. This means that you have to have the ability within your own personal circumstances to open the door when you hear the knock. By ability, I mean everything and anything related to your personal circumstances. If you are already underwater, don't take on more commitments.

But what often happens is that we hear the knock but don't believe we can respond. We aren't sure we can handle "it," whatever the new opportunity is. I hear frequently from professional women coaching other women that a common trait they see is a lack of confidence or sure-footedness—at least in how we speak and present ourselves. We may begin our sentences with "I know this is stupid," or "I am sorry, but . . . ," or some other verbiage that indicates uncertainty. Although I don't always agree with Amy Schumer, she has done a wonderful job of pointing this out in a very funny video involving professional women who apologize for everything. It's worth a watch, if you haven't already seen it.

As far as leadership goes, we women aren't always good about looking up to or selecting other women as leaders. A professor at the University of Texas told me about a class he conducts at the graduate level. In one instance, women and men were paired and asked to select a team leader. The team members were all equally bright with stellar resumes. In every instance, the women all selected men, and not a single woman was selected to lead a team. I know the women were up to the task, so something in the women themselves led them to vote for the men. Peer pressure? I don't know, but the fact that 100 percent of the women voted only for men struck me.

> *In my opinion, there still are not enough of these leadership positions occupied by women; but we'll keep working on that—together.*

What held the women back? Not enough self-assurance? Politeness? There weren't a lot of women in positions of work leadership early in my career. But that has changed in the last few decades, with much greater numbers of women working outside the home and in the boardrooms. In my opinion, there still are not enough of these leadership positions occupied by women; but we'll keep working on that—together.

If we don't believe we can perform a particular task, or accomplish a goal, then of course we can't and we won't. So if we don't see ourselves as capable of something, if we don't have an image of ourselves that shows us as fearless and willing to take risks, then we won't be there.

I think many of our limits are self-imposed. We see ourselves in one light, but perhaps others see us differently. Being introspective and analytical can persuade us, if we're lucky, to push ourselves out of our comfort zone.

If we are timid, how do we move ourselves forward into taking bigger and bolder steps? I mentioned earlier the episode of *Maude* that propelled me out of a rut and into another life and law school. A second incident took place some years later that changed my life once again in a major way. It turned me into a person I didn't know I could be. It started with a problem involving electricity on our own ranch.

*   *   *

Rural America largely receives electricity through power lines strung across the landscape. The Rural Electrification Administration started this process in the 1930s, going from state to state. The area where my family's ranch is didn't get electricity until about 1952, and the size, or transmission capacity, of the lines was somewhat small because of the lack of population. The Big Bend of Texas (so named because the Rio Grande makes a big curved bend there along the border with Mexico) is still considered remote, and Brewster County—where my family's ranch is located—is the largest county in the state, with a very low population-to-land-mass-ratio even today.

This ratio makes putting in power lines very expensive, because the ratepayers are few in number. In the late 1980s, shortly before my father's death, the local electric cooperative, which is a member-owned electrical utility (we call them co-ops for short) responsible for the lines, approached my father and me for a huge new right-of-way easement to build big new poles. Right-of-way for landowners meant we would sell an easement on the land to them at a reduced rate so they could use it to provide services to their customers. The existing transmission lines carried 69,000 volts or 69KV and the utility wanted to double that capacity to 138KV. That meant much taller poles, a substantially bigger impact on the landscape, and a much wider right-of-way. Going from a forty-foot pole to one over one hundred feet in height is quite a jump, and the easement would expand from twenty to as much as one hundred feet in width. The landscape and viewshed were going to change irrevocably. I wondered, *What was the need?*

My father and his father had routinely granted right-of-way easements over the years to the local power company so that we would have electricity. The first easements were twenty feet wide and had always been adequate. The ranch got electricity in 1952 and everyone was grateful for it.

Many ranchers in the area were deeply suspicious of the federal government. They were grateful for the roads and power, but the ability to have those roads and that power of necessity meant that some landowner had lost some ownership rights. Frequently, the price paid for the easement was miniscule in relation to the value of the assets received, but there was little or no controversy about it in the 1940s and '50s. But that didn't mean my father didn't have a strongly held view of his rights and the government's obligations—views that I certainly absorbed.

I knew nothing about utilities except how to pay our bills. I knew who our neighbors were down the highway toward the national park, and there wasn't any population to speak of on the east side of the mountains that would require this surge in capacity. Rather the opposite. Since the drought of the '50s, we had steadily lost people. The struggles to cope with the weather and still make a living off the land proved too much for many. The only growth was on the west side of the mountain range, straight down Highway 118 running south of Alpine.

I didn't understand why the co-op didn't just go down the highway using public right of way from the county seat, Alpine, to where the population growth was. Why were they making a giant detour through our land on the opposite side of a mountain range?

Going to law school gives you the chance to figure out how to do some basic research and so I called, made an appointment, and went to the Texas Public Utility Commission (PUC) engineering department in Austin to see if there was anything we could do that would make more sense, from both a financial and an engineering perspective. What did they know about the proposed new line? The shortest line between two points is still a straight one. The co-op proposal was a huge J-shaped fishhook with lines sputtering off the end due south of Alpine. The guy at the PUC didn't see why my alternative idea of running lines down Highway 118 from Alpine wouldn't work, and it would take the new power straight to where the supposed problem was. But of course it wasn't on the table—yet.

*He had essentially said I wasn't
smart enough to understand. A ratepayer and
a woman, I wasn't smart enough.*

When I raised the question in a local public meeting (which was convened to answer the ranchers' and ratepayers' questions) about changing the new power line route to a straighter course, the manager of the co-op said, "If I explained it to you, you wouldn't understand it."

Uh, what?

I couldn't believe it. He had essentially said I wasn't smart enough to understand. A ratepayer and a woman, I wasn't smart enough. Even if he explained it to me. But we certainly knew enough to write the checks to pay for the electricity. We should just sit still, believe whatever we were told about the route and cost, accept higher rates in our electrical bills, be smart enough to pay—but by his lights we were too dumb to ask questions. Or at least too dumb to understand his answers. His conception of the public being too dumb to know and understand, but plenty smart to pay, is prevalent in many taxing entities that I will talk about later. What disrespect to treat a member of the public with such disdain—and not even bother to hide it!

He made a mistake, a big one. He made me and a whole bunch of other people really mad. We decided, we ranchers in the far-flung reaches of a big state, to take him and the co-op on. The irony, of course, is that we were all going to be paying for the fancy opposing legal talent through our utility bills as they tried to squash us. The other projected cost we were trying to avoid was that of the proposed line itself, which, based on various projections, might cost as much as twelve million dollars stretched over time. This cost would be borne by about 3,500 residents, most of whom had very low incomes. No one could afford a costly mistake.

A rancher attorney friend of mine down the road, Ben Love, and I did all of the work ourselves to try to stop this new line. We were both lawyers and looked at this as an adventure. What did we know? Zip. But we were determined to learn. Our families and our kids got together often and it seemed like great fun. We went to the PUC; contacted big ratepayers (mostly related to oil companies in the region) who presumably would be interested in the issue; talked to groups interested in birds and scenic landscapes; and started to work.

We two ranchers had taken on a rural electric co-op, challenged its power line plans, and won.

I had just gotten my first computer and learned formatting. I was already a whiz-bang typist, so off we went. After months of prepping for and attending hearings, working with other lawyers, and writing briefs, we won handily by a 3:0 margin at the Public Utility Commission. The co-op's law firm charged $100,000 in fees, an enormous sum twenty years ago, and today as well. Our win made us happy, but as ratepayers of the utility, we still had to pay for the co-op's legal expenses. We essentially paid for them to be proven wrong.

We two ranchers had taken on a rural electric co-op, challenged its power line plans, and won. Sort of two Davids taking on Goliath. Some of our neighbors were mad that we hadn't listened to the more seasoned elders who surely were smarter than we were. Some across the state didn't like activist members who set a dangerous new precedent for other co-ops. Our names became well known in a select circle. But taking action became necessary in some co-ops when the board and management didn't serve the interests of the members.

As a result of our win, we decided to overturn the entire board. We accomplished this in three successive years by running a campaign against the incumbents who had been determined to stay with the manager. And the so-called multi-million-dollar problem was solved with a $75,000 transformer near the west side of Big Bend National Park. Today, in 2016, there is still no giant transmission line out there, and the population in forty-five years has only risen by about fifteen percent.

What did I learn? I knew nothing about politics or electricity, but I nonetheless learned that the little guy and little gal, the two of us rancher/lawyers, could take on a well-funded public utility and win.

We studied, learned, and formed coalitions. We didn't have role models for this specifically, but we had energy, belief in the rightness of our cause, and a great target that made us all fighting mad. Just mentioning the manager's name was enough to get me really fired up. Sometimes that is all it takes; but we do have to be educated, and role models certainly help. I never contemplated taking the co-op on at first, and I certainly had no idea about how it would end.

While my father would probably not have taken the action I did, I imagined during the several-year process that he would have been proud of my tenacity, my determination, and my commitment to protect our ranch—everything he taught me throughout his life.

Some of us may be fortunate enough to have our own personal kaleidoscope change lenses on us, giving us a tantalizing glimpse of a different future, as was my case with the co-op. I learned that I could do things I had never imagined, in a field entirely removed from my prior experience. I could be a female David taking on Goliath. I had done that to protect children in the courtrooms in Dallas, but this was a new arena. These images may be the key to our real, inner person. The warrior woman, the healer, the leader in her community. A different lens, in a different context, can change our lives in ways we would never have imagined. A new and different knock on our own personal door.

CHAPTER 7

The Tug of War—
Motherhood and Career

During the time I was ranching with my father and living in San Antonio, I was also trying to see if I could really fit in, since I hadn't lived there since high school, nearly twenty years earlier. In a sense, I was straddling two worlds: the one I had been raised in, where few women worked, and the one I had selected, where women worked and achieved in areas outside the home. It was challenging and I made a few misjudgments.

Birthday parties for our children are often cases where desperation leads to bad results. I wanted a great birthday party for our middle son and I didn't want to hire a clown, or get a pony, or anything fancy like that. I had always loved piñatas and felt that if I excelled in piñata selection, we would have a nice and fun birthday party for the children.

There were and still are lots of places in San Antonio (with its rich heritage connected to Mexico) to buy wonderful piñatas. I went downtown and found a huge white dog piñata, covered in curly white paper. Joe and I assembled the required tools: broom, rope, candy, and we were ready. Cake and drinks, napkins, and the rest of the essential cleanup items were ready, but the giant white dog piñata was going to be the star of the show.

The blindfolded children were ready to swing at the dog. I had seen plenty of piñatas in my time, and the candy explosion was usually readily attained. Not this time. The first boy swung, missed, swung again. *Thunk*. The dog resisted. The next kid came to bat as it were. Same sound. A thick thunk with no candy. I looked at another mother. What were we to do? How brutal could we be without terrorizing the kids and leaving them with nightmares? I took up the handle and flailed away, with more wrist action and a certain well-masked brute force. Nothing. We finally told the kids no more blindfolds; we were going to take this puppy down. I didn't use those words, of course, but we ended up having a jolly time extracting the candy and leaving a white shower of tissue paper in the yard. Lesson learned: If you want to run with the big dogs, get one that you can destroy—or at least understand your adversary. While I learned something valuable, I also learned that trying too hard to fit in meant that you often didn't. Either the piñata fit or it didn't.

My husband and I stayed in San Antonio for five years, where he worked in the high-tech sector, and I worked with my father. Joe and two partners, Larry Seligman and Michael Kenoyer, began to work on the creation of a videotelephone.

They worked nights and weekends at first. It then became clear that they needed to spend more time on the new venture. Joe had been working, when we first arrived in San Antonio, at Southwest Research Institute, a wonderful place doing very interesting research. But because of intellectual property issues as well as wanting to have a more flexible schedule, he decided to go back to teaching. He became a tenured Associate Professor of Computer Science at the University of Texas at San Antonio. He reduced his hours to half-time in order to work in the start-up for a year, while Larry and Michael were both full-time. At the end of the year, the three obtained venture capital financing and were asked to move to Austin for its greater high-tech labor force. I wondered how I could handle a longer commute to the ranch and San Antonio as I continued working with my father.

After the move to Austin, my work life became considerably more complicated. My father wanted me to come to the San Antonio office every day and I agreed. I also worked part-time at the same law firm where I had been employed for five years, plus I was doing a lot of volunteer work.

This period was extraordinarily stressful and I blame myself. I would get up about 4:30 a.m. (thankfully, we had wonderful babysitting help for the three boys), get breakfast, pack lunches for the boys, leave our home in Austin by six, and arrive in the law firm office in San Antonio about 7:30 a.m. I would work there until after lunch and then walk two blocks to my father's ranching office, where I would stay until it was time to drive back to Austin, often arriving home around 7:30 p.m. I was gone sometimes nearly fourteen hours every day. The shuttling back and forth between two cities eighty miles apart was a challenge. I loved it all: being a mother, a rancher, and a lawyer. The tough part was allocating my time so as not to shortchange any area of my life or obligations. I also had taken on several volunteer positions that I didn't want to give up, not wanting to think of myself as a quitter.

I thought I could handle it all without a problem. I was wrong. Sound familiar? That "quitter" word really wreaks havoc for us, doesn't it? We can raise a family, work, volunteer. We can do it all— just watch us!

Today I would say unequivocally that if you think you can have it all, you have another think coming. No one can give equal passion, energy, and time to the important areas of life. Joe kept telling me to drop something, yet I somehow felt trapped. I was the one constructing the trap. No one else.

Hindsight is always crystal clear and Joe was right. I was penalizing the most important areas of my life—my home, Joe, and the kids—for the sake of other areas and interests I just needed to drop. Undoubtedly, the travel time, gasoline, and stress all added up to both hidden and visible costs, which I didn't consider. Expectations I laid on myself were becoming a heavy burden.

We have to be bold when it comes to controlling our own destiny. I should have told my father I could drive from Austin to San Antonio only a few days a week, and done the same with the law firm. But I hadn't—again, not wanting to be a quitter. Then one day what I was doing to my family came home to me.

Alex, our oldest son, met me at the door as I arrived home after a full day's work. His birthday was in a few weeks. I was carrying one of those big, fat rectangular briefcases you see lawyers carrying, full of depositions and legal materials. He followed me into the kitchen. He asked if we could discuss his birthday party. "Not tonight," I responded. "I have a bunch to do."

He then asked, "What about tomorrow evening?" I told him I had to get all of the material in the briefcase read because I had depositions to worry about.

What he said then was eminently practical. "Can I make an appointment?"

A knife couldn't have hit my heart any harder. Appointment? What on earth was I doing? With that one question, everything became clear. I had forgotten my primary mission, which, in my view, was to be a mother to my three children. To this day, I am surprised and embarrassed at the clarity of vision his request provoked, and his need to even ask it.

Things had to change. I knew my father was going to be okay if I wasn't there as many hours every day. The law firm was going to survive without me. But I had spent all that time and effort becoming a lawyer—so how could I give it up? My self-image was partly based on being a lawyer; and I was a rancher in a largely man's world and it felt great. Could I make it work? I found out that I could have "it all," but that I just couldn't have it all at the same time.

Throughout all of this, Joe remained my staunch supporter, but he warned about the toll it was taking on us all. It wasn't easy on him, since he was the primary breadwinner; ranching wasn't exactly giving me a big income, and the expenses of going back and forth to San Antonio were eating up the legal income as well.

The next day I went to the law firm and announced that I needed to be with my children and that I would be leaving earlier each day in order to be home when they got off the bus. Everyone makes the choices that work for their particular situation. In my own case, I had seen so much in my years as a prosecutor that I honestly didn't feel what I was doing at the firm outweighed my obligations at home. I did the right thing for my family and me. I didn't get off the law escalator; I just switched to a shorter one. I have not forgotten that lesson that my son taught me; although subsequently, I did let it slip away for a while.

*   *   *

Along the lines of commuting, there is an entertaining story to share. Our third son, David, was born in San Antonio two years after I started working with my father. I nursed all three of my sons, and that posed its own challenges. Because I was actively running a ranching operation, I shuttled to and from the ranch from our home (in either San Antonio or Austin depending on which kid it was). It was a nearly four-hundred-mile drive from either city, and babies don't wait for rest stops.

I was in my late thirties, and as I was driving toward the ranch, I saw a highway patrol car sitting way off in the distance, and I figured if I stopped on the side of the road facing him, I would be able to feed the baby in peace. All was proceeding smoothly until the highway patrolman decided I must need help, since I was stopped on the road. He drove up, came alongside the passenger window, and stepped out of his car. Fortunately I had power windows, so I put down the window on his side.

"Everything ok, ma'am?"

"Yes, I am just nursing my baby."

He was wearing those beetle-eye reflective sunglasses, and he visibly started and stepped back. I swear he gulped, but that may be my faulty memory. In any event, he wheeled in his boots and retreated to his car and sped away. It's all part of what we do as moms. So what's the big deal?

Another part of being a mom is deciding whether or not to stay home, or work, or both. You will have challenges with any of these approaches, no matter which one you choose. For example, not too long ago I met with some women from various backgrounds who had decided to stay at home with their children. I don't for a moment think they regretted it, but they did experience some external pressures to be like other women of their age and educational achievement who had not stayed home with their children. What was fascinating about the conversation was that the "working" moms were also really struggling with their choice to not be with their kids, to not know what was going on in their children's lives, to not know what was in their backpacks.

As our children grow up, the fears about what
we don't know change but are still present.
We have to be strong for them.

Why is the backpack important? Because it contains everything your kid has experienced at school over a given period and is like a core sample from his or her life. As we parents try to set up our parental mining operations, we dig down deep in the backpack and find layers of dirt comingled with clues to their lives.

Okay. Two days ago the kid had a drama class. Rooting deeper you find a crumpled piece of paper with a note to himself to call someone about something or other. No date, but because it was farther down the mineshaft of life, it was probably earlier. And you didn't know anything about any of it.

The backpack is a real nightmare for a lot of mothers, as it is a symbol of what is really going on with your child. I include myself in that category. What in God's name was in that backpack? Did my kid launch a secret money-laundering scheme that I am too backward to recognize? A new Bitcoin enterprise? Or is it just full of sweaty clothes that I am going to want to remove with tongs? As our children grow up, the fears about what we don't know change but are still present. We have to be strong for them.

★   ★   ★

Shortly after September 11, 2001, our middle son was serving in the US Marine Corps in Anbar Province in Iraq. He was in his early twenties, and his job was to help clear the road of IEDs. I didn't know that's what he was doing at first, since information given to families was kept to a minimum. The night before the famous vote in Iraq when the fingers of voters were stained with ink to indicate they had voted, I got a call from him. It had been decided that each marine could call their family because the next day might be very difficult. I can still remember how I felt each time he called. I couldn't ask much, because he couldn't tell me anything. I couldn't reveal how frightened I was, because he needed to be boosted up, confident, and supported.

I kept my cell phone on at all times, since I might get a call at a weird time. My ability to focus on my job was very limited. As Agriculture Commissioner, I was in and out of the Texas capitol a lot at the time and had my daily duties to contend with, but there was nothing, absolutely nothing, more important than getting a call from my son. I could generally go about five minutes without thinking about him. He was on a nine-month deployment, and later we found out how many missions they went out on during that period, but we knew virtually nothing at the time. Actually, I am quite thankful we didn't know more. It was hard just knowing what we did.

I don't have any idea how mothers in the Roman Empire saw their sons go off to war and not return for years, if ever. We are both blessed and cursed with rapid communication. Why hasn't he called? How long has it been? I have the most enormous respect for women whose husbands and sons routinely deploy overseas and are in harm's way. They have extraordinary power—the power to be strong, the power to be supportive, and the power to embrace motherhood and their families.

You choose how and when
your next adventure occurs.

So, whatever decision we as women make for our careers, either as professionals or moms or both, that decision is the right one for you—and you can own that decision. There will still be opportunities if/when you decide to return to work outside the home. And with today's Internet commerce, flexibility in the workplace, and more men staying at home, there are many more options than we had just ten or twenty years ago. You choose how and when your next adventure occurs.

And speaking of the next adventure, I did something else after I moved to Austin. I wrote a romance novel of the very basic drugstore variety, and it was published a year or so after we moved. While I had always enjoyed writing, I didn't really settle down to it until after my father died and the commuting ended. Naturally I had shown brilliance by using my real name. I had no intention of ever being in public life, so who would care? As it turned out, some did. That novel was going to come up in the political arena in ways that I did not expect.

CHAPTER 8

Politics Ain't for Sissies

I remember my father once saying that old age isn't for sissies. I have modified his phrase to apply it to politics. Although he died before I got into politics, I imagine he would have uttered a few sardonic comments as I trudged through the halls of the capitol some years later.

Politics definitely isn't for sissies. It frequently turns into a combat sport, with bruising tumbles. It also holds the possibility of reputation destruction. A thick skin is very helpful.

Before I go on, you might ask: Why do we even care about politics? It's a good question, what with the cynicism and stalemates, and the media focus on all the things that can't or don't happen for the good of the American people because the parties are fighting one another. So, here's why: because ultimately every single thing in our lives, our country, our world, comes down to some kind of politics.

Every rule, every regulation, every kind of payment from a unit of government to us, or one from us to it, depends on some man or woman in a position of power over the public purse. So it behooves all of us to be serious about it and be engaged in what is happening.

You can't just ignore the whole subject and hope politics go away. They won't. Merriam-Webster defines politics as "the art or science of government, the art or science concerned with guiding or influencing governmental policy, or the art or science concerned with winning and holding control over a government."

The Urban Dictionary has a somewhat darker version when you look up politician—"A person who practices politics. 'Politics' is derived from 'poly' meaning 'many' and 'tics' meaning 'blood-sucking parasites.'"

I wouldn't go that far, but I have to say that I have seen aspects of people in elected office that I do not think reflect the best of our country. Facts matter, but I have seen instances where facts were ignored or shoved aside—all so one side could prevail. And prevailing meant getting their way, their tax, their privilege, their votes for reelection. This is a comment that applies to every political stripe possible—but I am not cynical enough to say everyone in politics is this way. So many people who sign up to serve and represent you and me are really great, honest, hard-working people who genuinely love the job and are public servants in the best sense of the phrase. And I am thankful for their time and work.

As a child, I was only somewhat aware of politics. My father, a Texan to the bone, was a conservative and a Republican. I was sitting in biology class at Vassar when we got the horrifying and terrible news that President Kennedy had been shot in Dallas. It was an absolute thunderbolt for all of us. Republican or Democrat labels didn't matter. The President had been shot and it happened in Texas. The name of the city, Dallas, kept cropping up, as in: "It could only have happened in Dallas." No other state or city would have let this happen. It isn't true, of course, but it left a dark, indelible stain on Dallas that is there to this day. "Yes, JFK was shot right over there," you hear people say. Tourists know exactly where it happened.

When I worked at the Dallas DA's office, my parking spot for the first couple of years was just past the School Book Depository. The grassy knoll was on my right as I walked to the office. I couldn't escape the memory. Nor can anyone today.

I worked for Dallas District Attorney Henry Wade as a prosecutor, and it was made clear we were all supposed to work for his reelection campaign. I walked door-to-door for the first time in my life. Dallas is hot in the summer, and we were starting the reelection effort in the hottest time of the year. I liked Mr. Wade enormously but wasn't happy that as a public employee I was pressured into working for him on his campaign. Nowadays this is not permitted, and there is much more scrutiny of the practice, which is good and right. But I did learn about going door-to-door, an experience that came in handy when it was time for me to do the same on my own behalf.

A year after my father's death, I was elected to the Texas and Southwestern Cattle Raisers Board of Directors. TSCRA was created in 1877 by a group of forty cattlemen who wanted to curb cattle theft and today has more than 15,000 members in Texas and the surrounding states. It's a strong and influential organization and a very important advocate for those in the cattle industry. I was one of only a couple of women to be so chosen. It was definitely a man's world at the time. But nonetheless, as a bona fide rancher, I was made very welcome. We ranchers talked about cattle, rain, water, grass, trucking, and a whole host of issues pertaining to our chosen livelihood.

Water was always a topic of much interest in the group and frequently the focus of potential legislation in the Texas legislature. The themes of conservation had direct meanings for us. We faced very different issues in the high desert than did ranchers in the piney woods of East Texas with its abundant water supplies; but access to and regulation of water were of real import to everyone—ranchers, farmers, and city dwellers, too. On our own ranch in West Texas, we always worried when the wind died, because when the windmill blades didn't turn, the water didn't get pumped, and we would then have to be careful about our water use. The presence or absence of wind was a major issue, unless you had another form of energy to lift water from the ground. When you spend a fair amount of time as a kid listening to water drip into a metal tank, you get a wholly different appreciation of its importance.

> *I think being an active and concerned citizen is something all of us should be—it's good for our own lives, but more importantly, it's great for our democracy.*

Because I was on the board of the Cattle Raisers, and because we had moved to Austin, the state capital, I was asked to testify before the Texas legislature on water issues. Proximity to the capitol didn't imply expertise, however. This was going to be entirely new for me. I was excited about learning something so different from what I had done previously, and which had the potential to get lawmakers to make changes that impacted the state's citizens. I had certainly grilled witnesses before in my legal career, but hadn't been on the receiving end of questions. I went to the Senate Natural Resource committee hearings. I learned the room number in which they were held, filled out the required witness card (they wanted to make certain you were truthful in your testimony, find out whom you were representing, and how to get in touch with you later). Then I waited for my turn to make comments to the committee and the nearly one hundred people in attendance. I continued to testify throughout the 1991 legislative session, which started in January and ended 140 days later. The session follows this same schedule every other year in Texas, so citizens and others have an opportunity to talk to lawmakers and participate fully in this legislative process. I had begun to figure out where things were in this law-making body and how things got done, but I certainly didn't envision myself as any kind of expert. I thought of myself as more of an active and concerned citizen. To this last point, I think being an active and concerned citizen is something all of us should be—it's good for our own lives, but more importantly, it's great for our democracy.

When I was asked by the TSCRA to think about helping in the capitol, I didn't know where to start. I called around Austin, joined another association related to farming and ranching, and followed in their footsteps. I needed an adult guide, and I was lucky to get one, a man from the Texas Farm Bureau. And it certainly helped that he was even taller than I was so we could keep pace with each other.

The very first day I walked into the capitol with my so-called guide, at the beginning of the 1991 legislative session, I was just beginning to learn where things were. After figuring out where to park and which door to use, we ran into a very tall man who grabbed me and gave me a big smacking kiss on the cheek. He was a complete stranger.

I had just met Edmund Kuempel, the state representative from the Seguin area of Texas. He was a big guy, with a broad face and a very friendly smile. I was in a dress with heels and we stood eye to eye. Texans are friendly, but this was unusual, even for Texas. I later called him Kissing Kuempel and found out he invariably kissed every woman he met on the cheek.

I asked around about him, because of the kiss. It turned out he was a staunch supporter of property rights, involved in protecting natural resources, and was a well-liked and respected member of the Texas House of Representatives. He just had that very distinctive quirk. This was the '90s, after all. What an introduction to Austin politics! He was definitely unforgettable, and he became one of my greatest allies and friends during my time in the Texas House.

Those first few months in the state capitol were eye openers. People walked quickly from place to place, then sat quietly in rooms where committees met. I saw state senators treat visitors and witnesses with great courtesy, as well as great disrespect. The political arena is filled with all kinds of people, as you might imagine. Some really care about what they are doing, knowing they were hired by the public to perform a task. Others seem to find the setting a great place to stroke their egos. Others just show up. The sausage gets made and the process is not always pretty.

*　　*　　*

A few days before the end of the 1991 legislative session, which had just completed its every-ten-year redistricting process, I was sitting in the gallery above the senate chamber when a friend of mine suggested I should run for the legislature. A new seat had been created in Austin, where I lived, and would favor a Republican. He said very memorably, "It will be a piece of cake." I thought, Okay, this sounds really interesting. I can participate more fully in this great process, listen to citizens, and propose laws I think will be helpful to citizens who want more access and understanding of their government. And I can advocate for ways to make government more responsive to the people of Texas. Great! And I am pretty fearless about new opportunities, right? Plus, I have a law degree, some work experience. Sure. I'll do it. It will be a piece of cake, right?

Not so fast.

What drove me to even consider running for office was that for years I had thought that government ought to be open, transparent, and accountable. In the ranching business, money was tight, and if you didn't have it, you didn't buy that truck, replace those several miles of fence, or get that year's dream object. But we depended on ourselves and were honest about our finances. To do anything else was to court disaster. But was the same true of our government?

Everyone should read Elmer Kelton's *The Time It Never Rained.* While it pertained to the drought of the fifties, he made the point that self-reliance and independence are worth more than nearly anything else. I think these qualities should apply to politicians as well. His book is about stoicism, endurance, optimism, not getting suckered, and not quitting. I liked it and wanted to be like the main character.

So why did I end up running for office? It wasn't just that someone told me it would be a piece of cake. The election process was certainly not. The primary was followed by a runoff, then a recount, then a lawsuit, and finally I won by two votes. But what did I want? Why do it?

I felt that things could be made better.

Obviously there were some real stars, people I admire today. But there were an unfortunate few whose power derived simply from longevity, and their lack of talent showed. I had been willing to fight for children as a prosecutor, and I said I would take that same energy and fight for Texans in District 47 in Austin.

First of all, I needed some real advice and help. I needed to run and win in the March Republican primary, and then I would be running against the Democratic candidate in the November general election. I was referred to a man named Bill Miller as a potential consultant. I went to meet him at his office on a Saturday in a downtown building. I could see his office with its door open at the end of the hall. Strangely, the ceiling literally appeared to have fallen in. The place looked pretty much of a mess. I wondered what on earth had gone on—and why someone had recommended this man to me as a consultant.

I walked in, introduced myself, and we shook hands. I had already sent him information about my background. He pointed to the ceiling and said, "I really need this consulting job." I must have looked shocked, because he started laughing uproariously, with a totally distinctive laugh—which made me laugh too, of course. I was to learn his laugh was one of the unique traits of this really talented man. Even thinking about it now makes me smile.

You have to feel that you are on a mission;
otherwise the process is too difficult.

Bill guided me through the campaign process and sent me to a campaign school for a couple of days. I had to learn how to ask for money, which is not for everyone, but absolutely necessary if you are going to run for public office. I have since become very adept. He and I formed a great bond, and I thoroughly enjoyed working with him. Through Bill, I met Lisa Woods, who worked for him at the time, and who has become a lifelong friend.

I was naïve, of course, but when I went campaigning door-to-door, I truly believed I could deliver things that people either wanted or needed. You have to feel that you are on a mission; otherwise the process is too difficult. It helped that I liked meeting new people and was spurred on by the possibility I really could help them.

When walking door-to-door and visiting with potential voters, you need three things: a way to be memorable, campaign materials to hand out, and a short speech that conveys everything you need to say about yourself, your views, and your experience.

I needed to be distinctive. I was tall, but the voters wouldn't have known that without seeing me in person. I needed something else. This was going to be quite a race for a very desirable legislative seat. What could I do? I had been in a parade once and watched a congressman throw plastic pickles out into the crowd, much to their delight. His name was Jake Pickle and he represented the Austin area in the United States Congress for over thirty years. If you are from Austin, you have probably seen his name on several buildings, and there is an elementary school in his name. The *eureka* moment arrived. The next business day I ordered a few thousand combs with my name on them. Combs handing out combs. I thought it was so clever. Over the years I have handed out probably 150,000 of these little treasures. Giving them to hair-challenged gentlemen was interesting, but they all seemed to have a great sense of humor about it!

Well, the lady energized the hell out of my hair.
Teased, backcombed, and sprayed, my hair
gained me three inches in height.

Every candidate had a push card to give to voters. It had a picture of the candidate, some relevant facts or position statements, and was meant to be immediately persuasive. You could also punch a small hole it, attach a rubber band, and hang it on a door for voters in case they weren't home when we came by—or, if they were hiding in a back room of their house waiting for us to leave them in peace. Bill decided he wanted me to have my hair and makeup professionally done for the photo on the push card.

The appointed hair and makeup day arrived. I submitted to the makeover and when I was able to see what I looked like, I was stunned. I was wearing a blue summer dress, which I had been advised would make me look energetic.

Well, the lady energized the hell out of my hair. Teased, backcombed, and sprayed, my hair gained me three inches in height. The eyes next. Blue eye shadow to match the dress. Lip gloss. Not the usual Susan look . . . at all. But I was running for public office and needed to look friendly and approachable.

*   *   *

Going door-to-door and handing out combs isn't always fun, but it's really important in an election and it's a great way to find out what is on the minds of the citizens you aim to represent.

I needed help of the most basic kind, and there were women in the district who offered it. I was overwhelmed with their kindness and support. Sometimes they would come to my house, sit at my dining table, and address invitations, work on maps for going door to door, and work on postcards. They also came to my small campaign office and worked the phones. Many of them were donors to my campaign. It was wonderful to be embraced and supported by these women—women supporting other women. Most of these women were in their late forties and early fifties and some older, but they all felt it was important to be part of the process. I could never have paid for the incredibly wonderful free labor these women provided. The majority of them were members of the Texas Federation of Republican Women, a grassroots community interested in electing Republicans and always helpful to women.

Interestingly, when I first ran for office, I was always told that women held a 3–4 percentage point advantage over men in elections. My own experience was a bit different. I ran against four men in the Republican primary and I towered over them all. "I am head and shoulders above all my opponents," I said. "I have the highest profile in the race." "All my opponents look up to me." I have a really bad habit of liking puns, and I uttered those phrases more than once, which didn't endear me to the men. But at least I was having fun. And I studied, learned, and prepared to deliver a speech conveying just enough information to be relevant in a short period of time—the elevator speech.

Politics is like being in sales—you are selling the notion that you can do things for the people who elect you, and part of running for office is the sheer retail nature of it. Retail means sales—and what you look like matters. When it is hotter than the hinges of hell and you are trying to convey coolness and calm at the front door of a prospective voter's door, well, it isn't easy.

Going door-to-door in sweltering heat knowing sweat is running down your back is not exactly the image of beauty you see on glossy magazine covers. I solved part of that problem by wearing white shirts, khaki skirts, and flats. The sweat was still there but mostly invisible.

I was trying to deliver some of my campaign materials to a door in a small community outside of Austin one day. A pickup truck was parked on the side of the street and as I approached the door, the sound of metal or a chain dragging caught my attention. The sound was getting louder and closer when a giant dog leaped out from under the truck, struggling to get to me and sink his teeth into my legs. Only the end of the chain held him back.

Yes, I was running. Running for office! I got the hell out of there. Not embarrassed much. Ever seen a cat fall wrong and then look around and glare? I suspect I did the same thing. Did anyone see me run? I left the next two streets off my door-to-door route.

Going to a door near dusk when you loom large is a challenge for the homeowner who might be unnerved at the long shadow. Because I was so tall I had to always stand back from the door.

The whole process of campaigning was daunting. I wasn't exactly a super chatty person, but I had to learn to tell my story, why I was running, and attempt to be memorable. I am grateful I was inspired by those plastic pickles and had my combs to rely on.

Another way to garner votes and get your message out is to attend functions or go where there are voters that you can approach. A memorable event occurred down in south Austin. On Friday nights at the Manchaca Fire Station there was a weekly fish fry, and the customers waiting in line often had a beer . . . or four . . . before picking up their food.

I had a stack of my push cards, which showed my photograph with that great new hair and makeup. I was ready with my elevator speech and my door-to-door speech, which had both worked well so far. I had not, however, previously dealt with the well-on-their-way-to-being-inebriated group.

I stated to one woman that I was running for district 47 in the Texas House of Representatives, and began to give my background. I explained that I was walking door-to-door, was a small business owner and former prosecutor, and hoped to get her support.

She stepped back and eyed me suspiciously. "Prostituter . . . walking door-to-door?"

It took me a minute to realize when I had said "prosecutor" she thought I was in a very different kind of business—on the other side of the law. I sputtered that I was former assistant district attorney—I threw people *in* jail—I was not a former prostitute!

I'm not sure what the economic model for door-to-door prostitution would have been, but it couldn't have been very lucrative. After that, I was careful never again to say "prosecutor." Lesson learned. I also believe the photo—the teased hair and brilliant blue eye shadow—gave the woman the wrong impression. We changed the picture.

The March primary ended with two out of the original five candidates in a runoff, and I had about forty-one percent of the votes going in. Then my opponent's political dump truck pulled up and unloaded all kinds of insane and negative stuff about me. I had preserved good manners and emphasized only the positive up to that point. However—negative stuff absolutely works. Time was so limited before the runoff that we didn't have enough of it (this was before Facebook and Twitter) to mount an effective reply. I could feel the mood shifting.

On the night of the runoff election, it looked as though I had lost by twenty-two votes. The next morning, I got up and sent letters to all of my supporters thanking them for their hard work and stating how much I had enjoyed the effort. It was not easy—it wasn't so much that I had lost, but that so many people had worked so, so hard to help me win. Some of these people I had just met, but they gave up every Saturday for months to walk door-to-door and encourage others to vote for me. Or they made phone calls to voters on my behalf, or mailed postcards to friends and neighbors asking for their votes. Some even sent me their hard-earned money to support the printing of push cards, to buy more combs, or pay a few of the campaign staff. It was a humbling and wholly unique experience. Literally, it took an entire army of people to get to election day. And although it appeared I had lost, I enjoyed the experience immensely, learned a lot, and believed I had made a bunch of friends.

But politics can often breed suckers. Through the years and through the elections, I have learned a few tough lessons. The morning after my supposed loss in the Republican primary, many of my so-called political friends vanished. I had written a winning and a losing version of my thank-you letter. My campaign director sent the "losing" version out the morning after the runoff, which was Wednesday. Instead of staying and doing the work she had agreed on, by Thursday morning she had cleaned out her desk, removed her family photos, and vamoosed. Gone. Adios. I had expected her to continue working for several weeks as we shut down the office because I was paying her to do so.

When it was discovered just two days later that there was a box of votes in a precinct that had not yet been counted, she called and wanted to know if I needed help. Thanks, but no thanks. On top of it all, I also discovered she had augmented her educational background on her résumé. I was dismayed but by that point unsurprised.

I very much place a premium on good, straightforward people, as we all should. How much does honesty cost? Not much. But, as I had learned from my father, the opposite is expensive—in life, friendships, jobs, happiness. That knowledge helped prepare me for the world I was about to step into—in ways I had not yet contemplated.

Yes, politics brings strange people to the table. But it also brings really good friends. That Thursday, before I realized there was still a chance for me in the runoff, I was walking in a parking lot from a local store. Toni Barcellona, a woman I have now known for over twenty years, was driving by and stopped to greet me really warmly. I needed a little TLC and she gave it! Not so the people who had been waiting for me to get power so I could help them in my new position. She was a friend who knew what it's like to have ups and downs. She is a strong, focused, honest person, and I am happy to say that she is very successful, still in her chosen arena, politics.

So, back to the votes. Two days after the election, a courthouse in a suburb in the district discovered a box of votes that had been locked up but never counted. This discovery was thanks to the keen observation of the teenaged son of the person who first encouraged me to run for office—Brad Shields, the guy in the Senate gallery who uttered the "piece of cake" phrase. The number of votes had been seen but not tallied for either the "winner" or me. I had to make a formal request for a recount and pay for it personally in order to even get the box opened. No, this was not 1948 in Duval County, Texas, where a box of ballots was "discovered," helping LBJ pull out a victory over Coke Stevenson for a congressional seat. This was 1992 in Travis County, and this was a legitimate discovery.

The recount showed that I had won by seven votes. Friends joked that my new name was Landslide Combs, modeled on Landslide Lyndon. My opponent said he wouldn't file a lawsuit, and that he believed I had won fair and square. Sure. At five minutes of five on the lawsuit-filing deadline, he filed a lawsuit. The claim was that Democrats had voted in their own primary, then crossed over to the Republican side to vote in our runoff, which is not allowed by law, and those votes would be discarded. They found fifteen individuals who had done that, subpoenaed them, and eight showed up for court.

My opponent clearly believed that I was the recipient of the Democrat votes. These voters were required under oath to state whom they had voted for, much to their collective outrage. He believed that I was going to lose votes because they would state they had voted for me. The first two stated they had voted for him, which meant that the math showed I had won by two votes. Yep, two votes. Needless to say, I was both elated and exhausted.

There was one other very bright spot. I was able to persuade Lisa Woods to return from out of state to came back and manage my fall general election campaign. I am eternally grateful for two reasons: She is super smart, capable, and disciplined and I have to thank her very much for all the campaigns we worked on together. And more importantly, she is one of my all-time best friends. When you can laugh with someone at all hours of the day and night, you have found a treasure.

About a year and a half later, I got a call from one of the two consultants for the opponent who had unloaded such nasty and dishonest things about me. He called to apologize, and said what he had done was unconscionable. I was floored. I was also touched that he cared enough about his integrity that he felt he needed to apologize. To this day, I think fondly of his courage, because it surely took some to call me up. The campaign they waged was really terrible—not just according to me but to others who witnessed it. The other consultant has never brought it up, and my opponent claimed he didn't know about it. Of course he did. We own our campaigns, as we own all of our actions in life. Saying he didn't was moral cowardice.

So there are good people, weak people, strong and honest people—individuals that pretty much reflect the population. The problem with the weak ones is that they often wield way too much power and are frequently held unaccountable. Remember this, and learn how to manage people who have these characteristics—it is critical to your success, and the rule applies across all sectors and areas.

Once the lawsuit was behind us, and the victory of the primary election was ours, it was time to focus on the November general election—which we won. Thanks again to an abundance of really great, determined, and generous people who gave all they had helping ensure a victory. Even though many of them are still my friends, I have lost contact with others over the years. But I want to thank each of them again here. The incredible experiences I had for twenty-plus years started in 1992 with all of them.

Saying "yes" and taking a risk can alter the direction of your life in very positive and powerful ways.

After the November victory, I remember feeling like I was a dog who had just caught the car (I actually envisioned a dog with teeth gripping a bumper for dear life) and we'd be at the Texas legislature in two months or so. The bumper was in my teeth and I was hanging on for a wild ride. One idle conversation above the Senate chamber had sent me in an entirely new direction. I had been asked and I had said "yes." Saying "yes" and taking a risk can alter the direction of your life in very positive and powerful ways.

*   *   *

An early glimpse of life as a freshman came unpleasantly. We were in the Insurance Building on the east side of the capitol while the new underground extension was being built. Freshman Dorm is what our two floors were named. I had found out how to get office furniture and met the wonderful woman in charge of the effort. She was delightful, I followed her every suggestion, and I was proud of my efforts to be early and organized. I got my furniture and it was delivered to my new office, which consisted of an open reception area, accessible to anyone, and two locked offices behind.

I went home that day feeling tired but successful. I had furniture, an office, and I was ready. Imagine how I felt the next morning when I arrived to find about half of my furniture had been stolen and moved to another freshman's office. The only reason I still had furniture in my back offices is because they had been locked. Wow.

I guess we were electing furniture crooks who decided it was easier to take other people's furniture instead of doing the work of finding their own chairs, tables, and the rare sofa. I never did find the furniture I had chosen and was forced to accept the junk the unknown thief had deposited in its place. I suspect they put my furniture inside their own offices and then promptly locked the doors. Lesson learned: Pledges of honesty and probity aren't always upheld.

Another incident, rather amusing, was receiving my first set of business cards as a state legislator. They came with my name printed at an angle. I asked if I were already being identified as a crooked legislator. Nervous laughter. The cards were reprinted promptly.

From such an inauspicious beginning, I nonetheless enjoyed that first legislative session. I met fascinating people from all parts of the state and from all walks of life. Women were powerful in that session. Libby Linebarger, from Austin, was chairman of the House Education Committee and she did a phenomenal job with a very difficult and contentious issue. She was unfailingly polite and although she and I were of different parties, I really liked and respected her. Senfronia Thompson, a legislator from Houston, was and still is a law unto herself. She also was a Democrat and ferociously focused, especially on an issue that had the potential to help so many Texas women. She wanted to pass a law on alimony and she finally got it done in the next session, as I remember. She was widely feared and widely respected. Republicans were a distinct minority. Later leaders such as Jane Nelson and Florence Shapiro in the Senate and Myra Crownover, Geanie Morrison, and Lois Kolkhorst in the House helped craft and pass landmark legislation.

But it is hard for women of both parties. Why? For many women, family concerns weighed on our minds. My three sons were only twenty-five minutes away, but others had to travel hours to be with their families. It was unmistakable that the toll taken on families was felt the most by women. Libby Linebarger, who was the mother of young twins, ultimately retired to be with her family. It was a hard decision, but I certainly understood it.

When I decided to run for office, I had high expectations. Smart ideas would have good outcomes. Reason would always prevail. What mattered was the power of ideas. Uh, not so fast.

My freshman year, I had managed to file several bills, and successfully get two of them out through their specific committee. The next step for the bills was to go through the Calendars Committee, which was like a cattle chute. What does that mean? Imagine that you have 15 or 20 committees, and about 5000 bills are filed. Not every one gets a hearing in committee because there simply isn't enough time. And often no committee member even wants the bill heard so it is dead anyway. And those that do get a hearing may not get voted out of committee and sent to the Calendars Committee, where there is a further winnowing because of the limited time on the House or Senate Floor and the logjam of bills piling up. The jam gets higher as the session comes to a close. That committee is truly a black box—what goes in may never, ever come out. And the process is very opaque. But I didn't know that at the time, due to my naïveté.

I just assumed my bills, which were perfect and brilliant, would sail through the process. On the ranch, every cow was finally accounted for, but to continue the analogy, in the legislature some "cows" went in, and a whole bunch disappeared. I solicited advice from a state representative named Robert Eckels from Houston who was on the committee. I asked him what to do to move my bills out of the Calendars Committee in order to get them in a position to be voted on the floor.

He told me, "Work the committee." What was that? He further explained, "Go see every member of the Calendars Committee and explain the bill to him or her and get feedback." I did exactly as he suggested. Muted responses. Then I decided to be memorable. I got index cards for each member, Scotch-taped a Jolly Rancher candy to each card (since I was a rancher, why not be jolly?) and wrote on the cards, "I hope you will think sweet thoughts" about the particular bill. My handwriting is normally pretty bad so I toiled over each one. All was going well until I got to the chairman of the committee, Mark Stiles. He was a tall, imposing figure, not known for suffering fools gladly.

"Combs, I don't like candy." That immediate response gave me pause.

"What would you prefer?"

"Chewing tobacco. Beechnut."

I stomped back to my office swearing I would never give in to that kind of nonsense. Two days later, the bill was still sitting in Calendars, so I asked a staffer to get me some Beechnut chewing tobacco. I handed over the money and hoped it would work. If I was going to have to play the game with vigor, I decided to up the ante. I asked the House photographer to document me giving the chewing tobacco to the chairman.

I wrote the bill numbers of both of my bills on the packet of Beechnut along with "Hi there, Mark," and some hearts and x's. I handed it to him and kissed his forehead way high up as the House photographer took our picture. Both bills were out of committee within forty-eight hours.

If the straightforward path won't work, get creative and go around it. If it's important, don't quit.

Another lesson learned. If the straightforward path won't work, get creative and go around it. If it's important, don't quit. I was not in the slightest embarrassed. I had learned that I needed to be creative and proactive if I wanted to get my two bills (out of the many thousands of bills in committees) out onto the House floor for a vote and keep them moving to passage. Pragmatism ruled the day. It was a very useful lesson for many areas—for that situation and different ones to come. There is usually some other way to get things done, even if at first you can't spot the solution.

The session wore on into the spring, and late-night committee meetings became the norm. Although I was only seeing my two sons still at home a couple of nights a week, I was able to make it up over the weekend. The third son was off at school at the Texas Academy of Math and Science in Denton and later in college.

We had pagers back then and my youngest son, David, learned how to have me paged. I remember being at the front mike on the House floor and feeling this weird buzz. It was the eleven-year-old. He missed me and it was hard for him. I was so glad I could be home every night, even if it was late. But it was difficult at times to balance being a mom and being at work. Two of the boys had birthdays during the session and I picked up their birthday cakes, a month apart, at 2:30 in the morning from the bakery in the Safeway grocery store. Thankfully, they were open at that time! But the good news was that the session was only every other year and then just 140 days long. For those of us who work jobs that don't have usual hours, it can be challenging. But somehow, we make it work, don't we?

*   *   *

Late in a legislative session, people are tired. It grinds on and a bit of light relief is welcome. Humor definitely has its place. A House member named Renato Cuellar had a whistle stashed in his desk, and several times during my first session, he would blow the whistle as a bill would come crashing down, brought down by a barrage of "No" votes. It sounded like a train whistle and it made all of us laugh.

Or the members of the House would poke fun at another House member who had written a poorly drafted bill. One of my long time friends, David Swinford, from a very rural part of the state, had written a bill about labeling seeds. As drafted, it would have meant that each and every single, individual seed would require its own label—instead of requiring the packaging to be labeled. Oops! Consternation ensued when he realized what he had done.

He went to the front mike where bills are presented and asked for everyone to vote against his bill. He then went to the back mike where you pose questions of the bill sponsor and asked the same again. An unusual request, to say the least.

The voting results are illustrated by lights on a big board at the front of the House. Green means "yes," red means "no," and white means "present not voting."

There was a wave of flickering lights. At first, the entire 150 votes showed bright green. David was getting panicky. He begged us to kill his bill. Then they all showed white or present not voting. David pleaded again for us to kill his bill. Finally, the board turned completely red. He was so relieved.

I found a lesson here too. Many of the House members have decades-long friendships. I certainly do. It was a good experience to be among colleagues, and we all supported one another when we could. We had to represent our districts and do right by our constituents, but we could also treat one another with respect, laugh, argue, and also remain friends. Yes, there were contentious times and plenty of disagreements, but the critical part of the work was that each of us was ultimately working together for the betterment of the state and its millions of citizens.

Occasionally the House floor could turn a bit weird. It turns out to be no surprise that men sometimes have a problem with women . . . about sex. Twenty-five years ago I decided to write a romance novel. I had read a whole slew of them, joined a writing group for input and advice, and forged ahead with writing it. I was totally surprised it got published under my own name—back in the late '80s. It wasn't a bodice ripper, just the kind of book that was sold back then in drugstores. I loved my characters. They talked and argued and did what they wanted and I kept typing, basically recording what they were saying. It was pretty much a cookie-cutter, Harlequin Romance–type book from years past. It wasn't a blockbuster, barn burner, or a bust. It almost paid the publisher back my small advance. When I had my incredible legislative primary, it didn't come up at all.

Remember, I had seen my share of calf castrations on the ranch and there was almost nothing anyone could say that would cause me embarrassment. I gave as good as I got.

Piece of advice, which bears repeating many, many times: Do not ever put your own name on a romance novel if you have any expectation of getting into politics. Or if you do, get ready to brave the comments and the harassment, mostly by the opposite sex. Printed copies of the chapter where man meets woman in the bedroom made the rounds while I was serving in the House of Representatives, and various chairmen of important committees thought it important to let me know they were reading it. I didn't feel it was sexist, just normal legislative harassment. The things the guys did to each other were phenomenal. This was pretty minor, and I thought it was funny. Remember, I had seen my share of calf castrations on the ranch and there was almost nothing anyone could say that would cause me embarrassment. I gave as good as I got.

The members were way too bored, and it was nearly the last week of the session. My major landmark legislation was on the House floor, ready to head to the Senate for the all-important final vote. I was defending it from the front microphone and then—a friend of mine, a state rep from Houston, strolled up to the questioner's microphone at the back of the chamber and asked:

"Representative Combs, do you feel a deep, burning, extraordinarily passionate desire to pass this bill?"

Huh? What was he talking about? Light dawned. The book. I had already been made aware that "the guys" were titillated by, well, mammaries. Guess that is where the adjective "titillated" comes from. I paused and then the devil made me do it.

Southern accent time. I put my hand to my throat, and told him, in the best, yet safest, imitation I could manage of Meg Ryan at the famous lunch scene, "Yes, I do. I would do just about anything for this bill." I tugged at the collar of my suit as though I were too hot. Heads were turning. No one around the floor had the foggiest idea about what was going on. The floor was silent. My friend smiled, said he liked the bill, and the bill passed.

One little problem. Unbeknownst to me, my husband and oldest son, just back from his third year at MIT, were in the audience, sitting up in the gallery. Yes, I had plenty to explain later. But it also showed my son I was a human, and that there is more than one way to handle harassment from others. Grace and humor come in handy when the situation is not too serious.

After all the fun and accomplishments I had while in the House of Representatives, I decided to run for higher statewide office, for the position of Agriculture Commissioner. All of a sudden my romance novel became a cause célèbre. I was proud I had decided to write a book and that I was able to get it published. What was the issue here, other than one chapter that talked about intimacy between two consenting adults? To a few people, it was a big deal and in a very icky way. Several male reporters got way too invested in talking about "the chapter" where "the scenes" were. I honestly believe one reporter from the Statesman had some kind of male-female troubles, because he displayed a near obsession with the book. He couldn't shut up about it. On and on. Good grief. He needed to get a real life. He implied there was something weird about me having written it, and he wrote about it repeatedly. The point, in his view, was that a woman who wrote this kind of book was of questionable worth. He didn't write about my qualifications for the higher office I was seeking with anywhere near the same zeal.

Another reporter, who positioned himself as hugely funny, basically said all romance novels were trash and women who read them were essentially dumb. Not that he used that word, but he belittled all readers and writers of the genre, which meant he was taking aim at women. Romance Writers of America took issue. Austin is a place that prides itself on being progressive, forward thinking. And generally people in Austin value women and advocate for equal rights. What on earth was going on now? Austin, twenty-first century, left of center, was showing nineteenth-century views of women, morality, and culture. Was it all just because I am a Republican? Maybe. But the deliberate contempt shown for women, the demeaning of them through the successful genre of romance novels, and the almost palpable dislike for me because I wrote a romance novel seemed heavy handed. As women, we can find a lot of different ways to manage these occurrences effectively—often through using humor in reverse—but we must also work to change attitudes and behavior, as should men. Period.

Juxtaposed with these ugly interactions was the fun I had with an editor some time later. I was in an editorial board interview with *The Dallas Morning News* while I was running for State Comptroller/ Treasurer in 2006. My Democratic opponent took verbal flight as he opined that there was no way I could ever hold any kind of responsible position since I had written the novel. I am not kidding. He hadn't read the book, as far as I know, but the newspaper articles describing my prose were quite lurid, once again picking up words and adjectives from the famous chapter. The opponent was horrified that such a book even existed, and he made it clear that I was therefore unfit for any kind of public office. The male newspaper editor continued to ask question after question, questions that I, as a former assistant district attorney, would call leading. My opponent took the bait and basically revealed that his entire campaign strategy was based on the book, and how it disqualified me from serving in public life.

Find your allies, and take no guff.

We finished the interview and the editor asked me to stay behind. He opened his jacket and, with a smile, removed from an inside pocket a copy of my book, which he asked me to autograph. I did, and thought it was pretty funny that he had deliberately and cleverly led my opponent to make those ridiculous remarks. He was supporting me in his own way. Sadly, I cannot say these kinds of interactions are unique to me. I think women face unfair judgments frequently. I say: Do as I did. Be strong and move ahead. Find your allies, and take no guff. As the author Alice Walker said, "The most common way people give up their power is by thinking they don't have any."

As it turned out, many of my former colleagues who'd waved around the burning hot, infamous chapter, asked me to send them a copy. I obliged, inscribing each one by name, noting that each man had been the inspiration for the book's hero, Ross, and that I was thinking of them when I wrote the character. Not true, of course, since I had written the book years earlier. But it seemed to be poetic justice. I wonder how many of them showed those inscriptions to their wives?

* * *

Women are generally believed by the public to be more honest and more ethical than men; whether or not we are too chicken to be crooked, we just aren't as bad as the guys. I personally like to think it is because we are more real-world—and we represent over half of the population, big chunks of the economy, and have to deal with families, work, communities, and so forth. I suspect we end up having to cover more of life's bases than the men, and being a bad player just takes up too much time.

Since politics involves power and money, it makes sense for women to be very attentive to the purse strings. We decide about home mortgages, car payments, student debt, and long-term financial issues for our family. If we have a significant other in our lives, we do those things in tandem. And whether you earn a lot or a little, or stay at home, these issues matter. The financial decisions we make have significant impacts in each of our lives, and the more we know, the better prepared we are for the inevitable unexpected events.

Politics can, of course, appear in our religious institutions, universities, schools, and communities. Any decision-making ultimately involves the art of politicking.

*   *   *

What do women need to do to be more effective power players? My own observation is that you have to always make allies, count your votes, work the "room," and keep on plugging. And maybe even jump into the arena yourself if you want to be an effective contributor to society in this way.

What is noteworthy in all of this experience is that some things don't change. More than twenty years later we are still debating about water, education, roads, you name it. So things get done and then undone. You win for a while, lose, get back up, and keep on going.

One more thing. Another significant part of this experience was that I was willing to jump in the ring. I was focused and pragmatic about it, I didn't give up, and I won. But I didn't just win an election that catapulted me into a whole new arena; I also fought and won to become a greater participant in what happens in our society—and to do it in a very different and amazing way.

I believe strongly that we need more women in the world of lawmaking and governing. In Texas, only about 22 percent of the members in the Texas State House and Senate are women—and only three of our thirty-six congressional members are women. Since Kay Bailey Hutchison retired from the US Senate, both of our US Senators are men. Yes, female numbers have risen over the past decades, but they are still not representative of the number of women in our state. Diversity in our representation is needed and critical—not only for the events occurring today, but also for the way those events impact the next generation.

We want our daughters, granddaughters, sisters, and others to know they can be a part of better governing—and they should be. So, for any woman out there now who is considering running for public office—be it for the local school board or a congressional seat—jump in. It is a lot of hard work, it will most likely not be a piece of cake, but you will love it, learn from it, and grow in incredible ways. Do it. Your community, state, and country are waiting for your leadership.

CHAPTER 9

Embrace What Happens and Make It Work for You

As I was nearing the end of my second legislative session in 1995, I realized that as far as I was concerned at the time, I had done what I set out to do. I had worked hard for my urban constituents all across the Austin and Travis County area, as well as those more rural areas, and had also gotten a couple of major pieces of legislation passed, all of which meant a lot to me.

The idea of staying in the Texas House for ten or twenty years just for the sake of staying did not appeal to me. I had seen too many people who simply . . . well . . . stayed. And stayed. The perks they got in Austin while in office clearly outweighed what the homefolks (their constituents) had; they didn't have much real power. A sense of entitlement crept in all too often for the elected group. The gap between those who stayed in office and the homefolks in the district, who operated in a different environment, often widened. Worse, the ability to comprehend what the average man or woman faced was all too often diminished the longer the individual stayed in politics. Or at least that is what I observed in a number of instances—not all, but many. There is sort of a feeling that "I'm special and therefore the rules don't apply to me." Sad but true in some cases.

The US Senator from Texas, Kay Bailey Hutchison, contacted me to become her state director at the end of my second legislative session, which meant that I would help her with policy, people, and issues across the state. I admired her a great deal and jumped at the chance.

As I look both backward and at the present,
I see a real disconnect between the elected class
and the people who voted them in.

I got a very eye-opening view of the job of a US senator and how she delivered real and effective constituent services across the state. She followed up on comments and questions from her town halls and meetings. The standard town hall was usually in a large meeting room, with rows of folding chairs. She would start off by giving a brief overview of what was going on in Washington and then take questions. Sometimes they were pointed; sometimes they were accolades. If something needed to be followed up, she always had her staff do it. Her belief was that the public was always entitled to a hearing and to her time. She had staff deal directly with questions both big and small. She did a fantastic job and I learned a lot.

As I look both backward and at the present, I see a real disconnect between the elected class and the people who voted them in. The dialogue we need sometimes becomes a monologue, and the voters become an afterthought—until elections come around and voters become front and center. Kay didn't operate that way. She worked hard and weekend after weekend came back to Texas from Washington to talk directly to voters across the state. She was proud of the fact that she went to each and every county.

She certainly was a role model—strong, smart, tenacious, and driven.

At that time our sons were growing up rapidly. Two were gone to college and one was entering high school. Joe's job had reduced his travel demands and so we were both around much of the time. I had very little travel that ever required me to be gone overnight. I thought I had left politics for good. I focused on the job with Kay and worked at the ranch on the weekends.

One thing I had learned in the legislative process was that the voice of the men and women who made their living off the land was becoming quieter.

Then Agriculture Commissioner Rick Perry announced that he was going to run for lieutenant governor, a very powerful post in Texas. Two different people approached me, suggesting I consider running to succeed him. It was an interesting prospect, a very important job, and I gave it a lot of thought.

One thing I had learned in the legislative process was that the voice of the men and women who made their living off the land was becoming quieter. Not silenced, but definitely quieter. In my second term in the Texas House, there were fewer than ten of us out of 150 House members who had a real economic connection to agriculture. That was astonishing.

Agriculture Commissioner is a statewide elected position, which meant I needed a working knowledge of a big state—254 counties and over 1,000 cities, and of the farmers and ranchers who were a critical part of our state's economy. Undoubtedly, my experience with Senator Hutchison helped answer my own questions about whether or not I could do it. But I still wanted to find out everything I could about the job.

I knew it entailed engaging with farmers and ranchers across the state, listening to the challenges they faced, and developing ways to assist them. Since I was one of them, I felt completely comfortable with that. If I were elected, I would be the first woman ever to fill the position, which at the time I didn't spend a lot of time thinking about. The job included a lot of regulatory functions, but also included helping farmers and ranchers obtain access to market, get brand recognition, and move up the economic scale. I believed that my legal and legislative background, along with my experience in New York, would enable me to fulfill the requirements.

My husband, Joe, and I talked about it. He thought I should do it and so did our sons. I met the Texas legislative requirements and decided to run. During the process, I found out a lot about how to put together a statewide organization. The first thing I did was to meet with people I knew who had statewide connections. I went to their offices, asked them to give me a list of names of other people I should call, and then put them all in a computer list. I then went through the list, day by day, week by week. I asked each person I called to give me more names. It was quite a project.

Jammies and computers are a great combo until you look in the mirror and scream.

I also enlisted the local Republican women for help once again, as well as those across the state. I ran this campaign on my own for about a year, using an empty bedroom downstairs in our home for my office. I made my own reservations, typed out my schedules, and kept notebooks full of lists. I am pretty much a list maniac. I still have notecards in the bathroom in a drawer so that if I get some late night or early morning inspiration, I write it down. As many of us know, having a home office is both a blessing and a curse. It is always available, which is both good and bad. Jammies and computers are a great combo until you look in the mirror and scream.

> *If you don't find such a passion and purpose,*
> *take a closer look and decide if the course*
> *you are taking is really for you.*

When you think about taking a job, running for elected office, or making a decision, find your passion and the purpose behind it. If you don't find such a passion and purpose, take a closer look and decide if the course you are taking is really for you. I stress this because there will be obstacles that you didn't expect for nearly any path you step onto. You could feel that you aren't really sure you can "do it"—whatever the task is. Unless you are focused on some purpose greater than yourself, you can get knocked off the path.

So why did I really run? Because I truly feared that rural Texas was going to be both silent and invisible and that it was going to be lost. I didn't know when I started out if anyone else would run in the primary, but I was willing to give it a shot—I cared about it, and believed I could outwork anyone. And the task was a big one. How many kids could tell you that the white fluffy stuff on plants is cotton and that it is eventually turned into blue jeans? Some children in Houston in the mid-nineties during the annual livestock and rodeo show were asked (I don't think this is apocryphal) where milk came from, and the answer was chickens. I heard over and over that when children were asked where an agricultural item came from, they said the grocery store—instead of linking the food to the animal or plant. And further, the last generation that was still connected to the land was just after World War II. The percentage of the American population that was in agriculture dropped from about 25% at the end of the war to where it is today, in the 4–5% range. Children weren't going to see grandparents on a farm or a ranch due to the enormous migration into our cities. They didn't see cows, sheep, horses, chicken, cotton, wheat—you name it. They saw instead packaging, bottles, and grocery stores—and of course TV commercials with jingles that showed the final product. At the very least, I wanted to keep the heritage of Texas alive.

I also liked the straightforward men and women of the land. They are wonderful friends and neighbors, and connecting with rural voters was easy for me. I spoke the language and was one of them. I could speak with real legitimacy about ranching in a dry area and hear what it was like in a wet one.

But why would the urban voter even listen? The shift from a rural to an urban population was nearly complete. Cities are where the votes were, but what could I say to the city folks to make them care, even just a bit, about the men and women of the land who were responsible for producing so many things they used every day? That's where my New York City advertising experience came in.

I would make the point that from the time they got up in the morning to the time they went to bed at night, everything they did involved agriculture. Their sheets and towels came from a cotton boll grown on a small green plant. Newspapers were derived from the pulp of trees grown in dense forests in East Texas. Breakfast, if it consisted of cereal, came from wheat or corn, eggs came from chickens, milk for their cereal came from cows. And on and on. Everything had some connection to a plant or animal grown or raised on a farm or ranch. Their clothes, every meal, all came from agriculture producers. For me it was so obvious, but I had been raised in and around it. What if you hadn't been? What if the folks from "The Beverly Hillbillies" were your only image of the source of America's food and fiber?

Agriculture in some form, whether direct or indirect, played a vital part in their lives. And I wanted them to know that their fellow Texans did a great job on the land and for the land. That respect for the land held by farmers and ranchers was both practical (the land needed to be nurtured for continuity), and passionate; because they loved it, loved its ability to live, produce, and create. I wanted to build the Texas brand so it would be recognizable and attractive—thereby ensuring that Texas farmers and ranchers would get a bigger share of the consumer-market pie.

My friend Lisa Woods had taken a different job while I was working for Senator Hutchison, and it took me a bit of time to persuade her to return for another campaign. But she did. We drove together all over the state—literally. We visited 250 of Texas's 254 counties, nearly all of them by car. I would pick her up well before daybreak and we would drive to four or five towns, do fund-raisers, meet with newspaper editors, and then crash. It was a lot of fun. The last event of the day was always over by seven; after that we might drive to a fast food joint and then tank up with gas to be ready for an early start the next day. The combs traveled well and I had adjusted both hair and makeup! I got to wear blue jeans, khakis, and boots quite a lot, along with nicer clothes for evening events, so I looked more suited to the position I was campaigning for.

> *Once elected, I set out with a grand vision—*
> *to ensure I failed no one, including myself.*

Although both of my parents had died by this time, I knew they would have been proud of my accomplishments—and they would have found it important that I pursue something that had such meaning and impact.

I won the election, beating a primary opponent and then one in the general election; and I became the first woman agriculture commissioner in Texas. I had faced only one opponent each in the primary and general election in the fall. (As it turns out, only fifteen states elect this position through statewide voting. There was a woman in

Iowa who was also elected.) It was a great adventure, and one that was close to my heart, given my family's ranching legacy; and—like the run for Texas House—it took a whole troop of volunteers, donors, drivers, organizers, and friends to make it a reality. The support from the agriculture organizations and individuals was amazing. I can't tell you how many people spent their weekends putting up giant 4' × 8' signs along Texas highways and country roads—they made an incredible difference in the outcome. I am truly thankful for everyone's trust and support, and it was inspiring to have so many people banding together for a common cause. Once elected, I set out with a grand vision—to ensure I failed no one, including myself.

* * *

For the first four-year term as agriculture commissioner, we worked on marketing Texas products and emphasizing rural economic development. Lisa Woods and I moved over to the agency to set up the transition team and lay out our program. The first major hire was the deputy agriculture commissioner, Martin Hubert. Martin had been working for then-Lt. Governor Bob Bullock when I asked him to be second-in-command at the agency. Martin is an Aggie, comes from a wonderfully successful and large ranching family in South Texas, and his experience in agriculture along with his brilliant legal mind made him perfect for this position. Martin's strong rural roots, combined with my background and Lisa's background and role as chief of staff, made us a great three-way executive team.

The flight from the farm to the city was producing well-known population losses out in the country. We focused on modernizing the agency, buying computers, and putting the regulatory divisions on handheld devices to improve efficiency and reduce driving time (which was an additional expense to the taxpayer, who was paying the freight).

We succeeded in saving money and being more efficient—thanks to an incredible, dedicated team. And that's what it took to be successful—an entire team of people, working together on a mission. And on a mission we were!

Every elected position has its own constituency—and its perks. Citrus—grapefruit in particular—is a big part of the Texas agriculture economy and we are justly proud of our citrus grown in the warm region of Texas known as the Valley. A state legislator from that area asked me to come down and ride in the citrus parade that was held annually.

> *My father might have described my face as "Looking like a jackass eating prickly pear."*

I was up for it. I arrived and discovered I was to ride high up on a truck just in front of a huge bed of citrus. Crowds lined the streets. I was urged by passersby to throw grapefruit to the crowd, but I figured I would knock someone unconscious if I ever let fly with one of the Ruby Reds. After the parade was over, we were handed a grapefruit pie by a woman I know well, and it looked delicious. We were supposed to be photographed eating the pie for the front page of the newspaper. The legislator backed away. It was left to me to uphold the honor of the industry. I was photographed with a luscious slice of pie on a plate heading straight to my gaping, open mouth. My father might have described my face as "Looking like a jackass eating prickly pear."

I was also offered other opportunities to have pictures taken which were to be memorable. The town of Sweetwater is famous for its Rattlesnake Roundup. As I recall, I was asked to give an evening speech to a large group about education, or economic development, or something. It was often common to receive something at the end—usually a plaque, a pen, or a book.

The emcee handed me a small square box and I saw the local photographer waiting below with a smile on his face. I became suspicious. Too much happiness. What was in the box? I figured they had stuffed some kind of rattlesnake in there and they wanted to see me jump or scream. Not going to happen.

I turned toward the audience, smiled widely as I lifted the lid, and then pulled out a coiled, stuffed baby snake about four inches high. I held it up next to my cheek, and that was the picture that made the paper. Mentally, I hoped that viewers would be able to tell the difference between a real snake and a politician selling snake oil.

You can literally survive just about anything.
Perseverance really does pay.

It seems strange looking back, but there was an accumulation of odd public events where I was photographed or filmed for TV in unusual situations. But it was an experience and all of it is memorable because it involved such great people.

I promise this is the last one, but it is illustrative of how you can literally survive just about anything. Perseverance really does pay. Economic development had been very important from the first day I arrived at the Department of Agriculture, and I visited various locales to discuss it. Frequently, there would be large Chamber of Commerce gatherings.

On this particular day, I had gone from Austin to Abilene by plane since the drive was about four hours and I was the scheduled luncheon speaker. It was a brisket lunch. I had made it a habit to ask to get my food early so I would be able to finish my lunch in time to make my remarks. The large room was full and there were probably in excess of three hundred people there, sitting at long, skinny tables, the kind you see in school gyms. The TV crews from two stations had arrived and were already set up. Often I would give an interview both before and after an event, depending on the sequence of the program. A congressman seated next to me asked me a question. I had already cut off a piece of brisket, which, by the way, looked delicious, and stuffed it into my mouth. Literally.

I tried to chew so I could answer. Not happening. The brisket was stuck and it seemed to swell in my mouth. At first I didn't realize I wasn't breathing. It took a couple of seconds for me to understand. The congressman got up and backed away. Guess he didn't want to be within projectile range, assuming I might expel it.

My face must have turned white, and I clutched my throat. Someone at the table knew I needed the Heimlich maneuver. There was some chaos and consternation. I was still not breathing, and I really did think this might end unpleasantly. No one at the table offered to help, and I didn't see anyone coming forward. There was someone yelling, "Is there a doctor in the house?"

I stood up so that if they found someone, they could stand behind me and get at my diaphragm. A nice (but short) guy showed up after what seemed like an eternity. I do not think he was a doctor, but he was connected in some way to the health field. I had been in heels, so I had to bend my knees so he could get to my midsection. He was talking to me but I wasn't listening too well, as I continued to try to get the meat to go either up or down. He pumped hard twice on my stomach and the meat flew out. Captured on TV by both cameras!

I probably looked ghastly. I was asked if I wanted to leave or go ahead with the program. I said just give me a minute. Lipstick, blush, a big drink of iced tea, and I was back in the game. I stood up, went behind the podium, and said, "I will nearly give my life for the beef industry, but not totally." Standing ovation, and then I launched into my speech.

What about the TV footage? We called the first station and they said they had pulled it. The second said they would run it. "Still Alive at Five" could have been a nice introduction. Makes me realize that the media has an inexorable march toward the public, no matter how you may feel about it. But today with the ever-present high-tech phone, anything you do or say can be instantly viral. So pay attention.

Lesson learned: I should have listened to my grandmother, who had told me as a child that I needed to "fletcherize" my food. It basically meant chewing each bite over twenty times, grinding it into tastelessness. After this, I learned how to administer the Heimlich to myself over the back of a chair. If you are out in the middle of the boonies, as I was at the ranch, with no nearby medical care, you get proactive.

I also learned that you have to push on past disasters. My first marriage had certainly shown me that, along with the near-loss in my first race for the Texas House—and so did this. I really had thought I might be a goner. But no: I was still alive at five.

*　　*　　*

We created the Go Texan marketing campaign and brand during our first six months in office and it continues today. It's something I am very proud of. Tommy Lee Jones did a wonderful TV commercial for us, as did the famous baseball player Nolan Ryan. Having two such powerful brand ambassadors raised the profile of every farming and ranching family. They became more real. And both Tommy Lee and

Nolan did it for free! There were many other successes, all fueled by a strong vision, supportive community, and amazing staff. It was an incredible time, and we all agree, even now, it was quite exceptional. For instance, we discovered that by raising the profile of a particular product, more sales were made, which meant that a particular family achieved more success and so did their home community. Rural Texas was getting a much-needed boost in the arm. We also took the agency from a place with few computers to an agency where everyone had a computer. We streamlined all processes, merged data systems, and saved money. Millions of dollars. It was a real blast, and the team at the agency could feel the pride that the legislative branch had in their work.

*　*　*

My first four years as Texas agriculture commissioner zipped by, but I felt I needed to do more. In 2002, I ran for re-election and won again by a large margin. It was great and I was energized!

My second term would build on what I had accomplished in the first, but my focus was now on children and nutrition. Because farmers and ranchers provide food, it seemed to me that a natural tie-in with the urban public was through how we fed our kids. Small towns often are starved for resources but full of small town can-do spirit that I hoped could help me. I wanted to take on the junk food that was in Texas public schools. Soft drink companies had given lots of money to public schools in exchange for branding rights—on the scoreboards, on the drink machines lining the halls, and in various ways to support athletics. I believed the return to the soft drink companies such as Coca-Cola, Pepsi, and Dr Pepper was many times bigger than they paid for the logo display because of the value of the branding opportunity.

Schools became addicted to the cash and
appeared deaf to entreaties to put children first.

When I had been an assistant district attorney in Dallas handling child abuse cases, neglect and starvation were what we battled. It seemed to me that we were now feeding our kids to an early grave. So what was happening? Our kids were terribly unhealthy. We were seeing children under the age of ten being diagnosed with type 2 (adult-onset) diabetes.

It felt like I was coming home, turning my attention once again to children. The fuel that had made me work so hard for those abused children in Dallas came to life again when I saw how we, as adults, were abusing kids for our own financial gain in our schools. By abusing I mean feeding (selling) them copious quantities of junk so that someone could get rich off the sales. Schools became addicted to the cash and appeared deaf to entreaties to put children first.

The legislative drubbing a few of us took in 2003 when we tried to address this issue was a real eye-opener. I thought back to my days as a House member and fondly recalled the passion and energy shown then by so many to help their fellow Texans. Why not the children?

I hoped that legislators would care about my new cause, believing that we needed to take action to create healthy school environments. I found two legislators to carry bills that would clean up our schools and put an end to kids acting as ATMs for businesses inside schools. Great ideas, great bills, worthy causes—we ran smack dab up against big soda companies.

The exclusive beverage contracts they had with the public schools actually gave the schools more money as a share of the sales if the kids drank a twenty-ounce soft drink rather than the water sold in the machines. Water produced less revenue. I asked representatives from a soft drink company who came to see me why water produced less revenue and was told it was because they had to do more to make the water drinkable. Really? So the water in a soft drink is dirtier? That exchange didn't go well. I kept hearing school officials and school board members—who should have kept a watchful eye on our children—saying that they needed to do whatever it took to get money into the schools, even if it risked the health of their children. That was awful.

The stats we had showed that African-American and Hispanic children were most likely to end up obese because of a genetic predisposition. Our health commissioner at the time, Dr. Eduardo Sanchez, who is still an impassioned advocate for children and their health, put it this way: Genetics loads the gun, behavior pulls the trigger. He worked tirelessly to help these children.

We hoped that the minority House members would hear our message, but we were not successful. The legislative session ended with the bill never getting out of committee in either the House or the Senate.

Everything happened behind closed doors—there were few witnesses who openly signed a witness card and testified against the kids. Strong support for the kids was openly shown by a nurses association and the state PTA. The entire health community was on the side of the kids. But superintendents weren't. Soft drink companies weren't. Candy companies weren't. I had learned by then that hearings where people testified for and against various proposals were just the tip of the iceberg. Many times there were stealth attacks behind closed doors. That is what happened to us in 2003. We had the right idea but didn't have enough allies.

This was where we needed strategy and creativity—both of which work in all kinds of situations to help claim victory while preserving integrity.

*One week later, I sent out a letter to every
school district in the state informing them
that the old days were over.*

Earlier that year, I learned that New Jersey had figured out a way
to start the process to get healthier foods into schools. They asked
their governor to request that the United States Department of Agriculture move their lunch program (it involves federal reimbursement
dollars) from the state education agency overseeing the schools to the
agriculture commissioner. This sounded like a good backup plan for
us. Our then-governor, Rick Perry, was wholly supportive. We sent
the request to USDA; they executed a quick turnaround because we
had already discussed the idea at various levels in the federal agency
and the support had been given. The Texas Department of Agriculture
received the authority to run the Child Nutrition Program on July 17,
2003, only about six weeks after the end of the legislative session.
One week later, I sent out a letter to every school district in the state
informing them that the old days were over. The soft drink companies and superintendents were horrified—they thought they had won
when no nutrition bill passed before the legislative session ended.

*I knew I was doing something right,
considering the level of anger that was generated.*

When the word got out, you would have thought I was the mean-
est woman on the planet. I received letters, over a thousand emails,
phone calls, and the newspapers across the state had a field day. How
dare I? Nanny state! Evil bureaucrat! Cupcake Nazi! (That was a personal favorite.) I knew I was doing something right, considering the
level of anger that was generated.

From 2003 through 2006, we made sweeping changes to portion sizes and amounts of sugar and restricted the availability of foods of minimal nutritional value. We got rid of fryers, mandating that schools had until 2009 to start baking their potato selections. Pizza Hut even changed its pizza recipe to comply with the Texas model. Why? Because we ran the largest school breakfast and lunch program in the country.

Time magazine ran a story in 2004 calling me "The Cafeteria Crusader" and noted how prevalent the practice was of selling candy to kids so that the schools could buy VCRs and other classroom items. The fact that a national magazine wrote about the food fight was important in setting a national tone. Michelle Obama, years later, followed suit in her efforts to bring changes to schools.

Was it easy? No. I received hundreds of very angry, vitriolic emails— they suggested I assume certain body positions requiring contortions worthy of really late night comedy or other kinds of shows that I don't watch. There were no direct threats but the tone was very strong. There were some nice and laudatory emails, but at first the numbers were heavily tilted toward the opponents. We answered each and every email and letter, and persevered. It was a very difficult time for the staff. They hated answering the phone and hearing people scream at them when they knew they were trying to help the children of the state. Two years later the anger was gone; moms who had worried about what their kids were eating were happy. Soft drink companies heard the distant rumblings of the demise of fatty foods, and they began to think about ways to modify their offerings into this captive audience of five million kids. Schools still weren't necessarily on board, since they were still selling candy to elementary school kids to bring in more cash.

Don't give up. Be fair, but be persistent—
and know when to change course.

A couple of points here: Sometimes politicians can be more swayed by those who give them political contributions than they are by the larger policy issues, such as children's health. This is true of both major parties. I couldn't get real support from either in the legislature. Second point: If one way doesn't work, see if you can find another. Don't quit! I mean that. If going in the front door doesn't work, try the side door, find a tunnel, find a new building. In our case, the new "building" was going around the legislature entirely and doing it by moving the program from an agency that wasn't going to back it to one that would. This helps in all kinds of situations, not just politics. Try it with your kids, your conversations when asking for a raise, or interviewing for a promotion. Don't give up. Be fair, but be persistent—and know when to change course.

*　*　*

Then came January of 2015. The newly elected agriculture commissioner—in his first week—announced that freedom to have French fries and cupcakes was the most important work in his new job. He was going to undo the work on children's nutrition that had been so painfully achieved over an eleven-year period, dating back to 2003. Why? As far as I knew, the press had been favorable for years on the Texas lunch and breakfast program. The health community was on board, and the parental landscape had changed—so I didn't know what the reason could possibly be to attempt to reverse course. Evidently, according to press reports, he had heard from "some" folks.

I don't think he cared about the kids, their health, or anything else. I have long believed that we elect the people we deserve. He is someone I clearly do not admire. But more importantly, I just can't understand why he didn't put the health of our kids before some publicity stunt. The good news was that the decade of high nutrition standards had already done its persuasive work, and most schools resisted his call to roll back the standards. The *Time* article was hugely helpful— and illustrates the important fact that policy changes can benefit from public awareness.

Take on the fight in the arena
closest to you. Don't quit! Get creative!

You may be angry and perhaps sad about this man's intentions, but if you want to get something done, prepare for setbacks, prepare a way to get around them, and if necessary go to the closest level of action where you can be successful. In this particular instance, that would have been at the individual school level. Take on the fight in the arena closest to you. Don't quit! Get creative!

Making policy changes can be daunting. But I would argue that women are very good at making them. We are willing and very good at working for consensus, and then being bold when we have to skirt the normal process. This is where flexibility and focus come in. As I have said many times, you must be willing to keep looking for different doors, different routes to success. When our goal is protecting children, being fearless about helping is the only option.

Politics is a combat sport, and certainly fearlessness is required, but so is the long view and a healthy sense of humor. It keeps the negativity at bay and lets you get up, ready to keep on marching the next day. Maybe you work in a similar environment and can see the parallels.

A takeaway from all this is that we women need to actively work to control our own destiny. I deliberately decided to run for office, even though I had only a dim understanding of what it might entail. But I was willing to take a risk in order to achieve something. We don't always know what we want to do, or whom we want to be at any particular moment, but we can always benefit by thinking carefully about it.

But do we actually think about what kind of human we want to be? Do we then—with deliberate and careful consideration—turn ourselves into that individual?

Some years ago, I read a novel by Thomas Perry. The mother of the heroine came from a mysterious background she never spoke of, and which she had left far behind. She decided she was going to become a totally new person. She did everything she knew how to make that transformation until she turned into that woman. She became a great mother, a loving wife, and one of the most admired people in her community. It was clear that the new person was vastly different from the earlier model. Hints were made that she had somehow been connected to a crime-world figure and had escaped, but details were sketchy. However, the emphasis in describing her efforts to change made the point. Wherever she had come from, it had been dark and dangerous, and she deliberately moved from night to a much brighter day.

Most of us don't plan with that kind of intentionality or over the long term. We may plan for this evening or that meeting tomorrow, or we may think about furthering our education or looking for a better job. But do we actually think about what kind of human we want to be? Do we then—with deliberate and careful consideration—turn ourselves into that individual? It is up to us to craft that person, find that sense of will and purpose, and keep our eyes straight ahead.

Are we going to be deliberate and bold about our aims? Are we going to crumble at the first sight of opposition or are we going to somehow become steel-willed and keep moving forward?

As a kid, I was terrified of shots. Polio had been a real problem in San Antonio, and prior to the Salk vaccine, a series of very painful shots were given to kids. Also, because the ranch had nails and manure, we got tetanus and typhoid shots. I was a complete crybaby, and it undoubtedly annoyed my mother, who spoke the famously incorrect words, "Susan, this is going to hurt me more than it hurts you." But one day, I decided that on a certain date shots were never ever going to bother me again. I went from giant sissy to at least normal person because I willed it, and because I was also so embarrassed about tearing up. I was probably about ten, way too old to be such a baby, and yet old enough to know I could change. I suspect part of the reason I was such a sissy was also because my mother wouldn't warn me—she would just pick me up from school and we would then zoom down to the doctor's office. No preparation. But I finally decided to grow up.

That's it. I willed it. Just try it. You will be amazed at the outcomes. Capture whatever embarrassment or disappointment you're having, and turn it around.

Ask the young kid who is going down the bunny slope on snow skis for the first time how he or she feels. Perhaps they're terrified, but they're also so proud that they are going to go back up that hill until they can get it done. They're too young to know about giving up. No one has yet knocked the bright shiny hopes out of them.

Our oldest son was six years old when he was given a computer game involving the perils of Princess Sabrina. If she was not saved by dawn, she would die. No one had told Alex that he was too young to succeed at the game. At the same time he was working to win at the game, a lawyer at the firm in San Antonio where I was working was trying to win as well. When I came into the office one day and told him Alex had won and saved Princess Sabrina, he was amazed. "How did he do it?" he asked. I didn't have any answer except that no one had told our six-year-old he might fail . . . so he didn't! The messages we give our children, our boys and girls, need to expand their horizons, not narrow them.

The same is true for the messages we give ourselves.

Many women are quietly courageous, even heroic. Across the world, they face extraordinary hardship and yet they don't give up; they continue on. Eleanor Roosevelt was a woman whose accomplishments are too numerous to list and who showed courage in immeasurable ways. One time stands out for me in particular. In 1939, the African-American contralto opera singer Marian Anderson asked to sing at Constitution Hall, as part of Howard University's annual fundraiser. Washington, DC, was still very much racially segregated at the time, and the group who owned and controlled Constitution Hall would not allow Ms. Anderson to perform. The First Lady was undeterred and eventually brought Ms. Anderson to the capitol to perform at an outdoor concert at the Lincoln Memorial. An estimated seventy thousand people attended, and it is remembered as a watershed moment in the civil rights movement.

In the words of Eleanor Roosevelt, "You gain strength, courage, and confidence by every experience in which you really stop to look fear in the face. You are able to say to yourself, 'I lived through this horror. I can take the next thing that comes along.'" Amen to that— and you can, too.

I think about our own country's history and am reminded of Elizabeth Cady Stanton. Possibly you learned about her in your high school history class. She lived in the 1800s and was a wife, a mother, and a serious activist who is credited with starting the women's suffrage movement. Certainly this was not an easy undertaking. In her words: "The best protection any woman can have . . . is courage."

Read those words both silently and aloud, and then ask yourself how they apply to you. To anyone you know. How can you make them live for you? Life is for living to the fullest—and making the moments and our actions hold meaning—in whatever way we define meaning. It's inside all of us. Embrace it.

CHAPTER 10

It's Their Money

Courage. We all have it and can choose to use it at any time. I actually thought about this as I contemplated moving into the next phase of my professional life. Two four-year terms as agriculture commissioner seemed sufficient to accomplish the goals I had set out, and I was ready for a new challenge. An opening for the office of comptroller of the state sounded fascinating. The job of comptroller is a big one, as it contains the Office of Treasurer, which was moved to combine with comptroller in 1995. The position also is the tax collector for the state; it's basically the CFO of the state with a myriad of data-reporting responsibilities. Would I be up to the challenge? Could I stretch myself for such a next step? I had met a great friend, a political consultant named Reggie Bashur, a couple of years before. He encouraged me to take it on. Faith in yourself is always critical, but so is help from a third person.

The election in 2006 was fairly routine, except for the process of going through editorial boards to be vetted. As I mentioned earlier, my opponent for comptroller in the general election thought because I had written a "steamy" novel I was unfit for any kind of public office. (That was the time one of the newspaper editors sitting in on the interview had a copy of my novel tucked away in his jacket and was deliberately leading the guy on. At his request after the interview, I autographed it.)

I won the election handily, was ready for the new challenge. (I still get requests for copies of the book, and can't resist inscribing them "Fondly" to the recipient.)

During my first four years as comptroller, I set forth a vision of open government—complete transparency—and I pursued efforts to ensure that we got the best dollar return for the taxpayers. In order to do that, we had to know how the three-thousand-person agency ran, how the functions were assigned, and whether we could find some efficiencies inside and between divisions. Martin Hubert and Lisa Woods, along with many of the great directors of the comptroller's office, joined in the effort, which was the only way I could imagine making it work. They worked tirelessly—we all arrived early, stayed late, and worked weekends. A big agency, with big tasks.

This all can seem kind of boring unless you think about it in the context of not quitting, not giving up, and being determined to make something better. It is very difficult to get people to change to a new way of doing things, even if you are convinced there are serious positive benefits. I tried first to change the way of thinking and had a couple of banners made that said SIMPLER. SMARTER. FASTER. If you aren't going to get more people or money to do more tasks, you have to figure out a better way to do it. So it has to be simpler, smarter, and faster. I had learned that from the ranch.

Ultimately we saved about twelve million dollars in the first five years, with over half of it in the first two.

Government agencies don't often think about being either horizontally or vertically efficient. Fiefdoms develop and managers clutch their projects to their chests, refusing to let go. That usually means more money is spent than necessary. We discovered a number of examples of this. Various divisions bought their own printer toner cartridges on a multitude of contracts instead of using the buying power of the entire agency and negotiating a better price. The agency hadn't employed strategic sourcing, which relied on economies of scale to derive value. In fact, few agencies did that kind of purchasing. It was a lot of fun ferreting out ways to bundle purchasing and save money, and it took a lot of great minds within the agency to make this work. Ultimately we saved about twelve million dollars in the first five years, with over half of it in the first two.

We were receiving color-coded envelopes, allotted to the various taxes that were being paid. One morning I went up to the mail sorting room in order to better understand the process. There was a long U-shaped table with a conveyor belt. Envelopes were being dumped on it and then going through sorter machines. A couple of them flew off the end as the table curved—right where I was standing. Staff had to get to the office early to sort the mail, and then get the envelopes distributed to the right individuals in the various tax divisions for further routing.

Something occurred to me. Didn't the United States Postal Service still sort mail? Research ensued. Yes. So we got separate post office boxes for each tax type, and the mail arrived at our building presorted. We ended up saving $328,000 because we didn't have to buy a new sorting machine. Simple idea and it saved money, which was part of our goal, since we were handling the public's money. Another lesson learned from the ranch.

Another thing I learned was that merely recognizing that there is a better way won't necessarily persuade everyone. If they have always done it one way, to some that is the best way.

We cleaned up our own expenses internally and then wondered

164 | TEXAS TENACITY

about spending patterns across all state agencies. Billions were being spent purchasing goods and services. I questioned if there were any economies of scales we were missing. If we heard that other states had better and more innovative processes, we sent people there to investigate. Copying great methods is very efficient. We discovered, for example, that we were paying more for Dell computers than Florida was—same company, same model computer. We just hadn't worked hard enough to get the same deal. We also discovered a company that added on a percentage for office supplies being purchased by state agencies, which that company obtained from a large standard office supply company. They didn't want their money pipeline disturbed. The taxpayer was and would not well represented unless we could honestly get a grip on spending.

There were billions spent all across our large state through a variety of agency pipelines, and access to those lucrative contracts was a powerful inducement for the vendors doing business with the state to hire lobbyists to oppose any change in the process. I had campaigned for the comptroller job based on the notion that the state needed what amounted to a single set of books. There were dozens and dozens of agencies with different reporting systems, and it was virtually impossible to aggregate the information in a cohesive way in order to see what was actually going on across the state. Instead, the state legislators only got spending information one agency at a time, and it wasn't really aggregated, so duplications could be found. As my father would have said, this project became a big burr under my saddle. It was equally irritating that it was proving to be an uphill battle too. But we ultimately won.

We were able to get a bill passed in the legislature that gave the comptroller's office the right to start compiling a single set of books, meaning we would be able to make each agency report in a single format so that comparisons could be made and duplications erased.

Is this exciting? Maybe not to the ordinary citizen. Unless you realize that maybe, just maybe, *you* can find out what the heck is going on with your money—and save some in the process. And sometimes the saving of money by the state translates into lower taxes in the future with the same level of services. By the time I had embarked on my second term, I thought I needed to find out more about local government entities.

What if you want to really do something good? Like, maybe tell the truth about debt that is owed by the public entities around you? Schools? Cities? Counties? After all, it's our tax money that supports all of these entities, both at the state and federal levels.

Gina Raimondo, then treasurer of Rhode Island, was faced with serious pension problems in late 2011. She was facing powerful forces—unions in particular. She saw that the path to sustainability would require modifications of pensions, because left unchecked, the cost for the pensions was going to encroach on monies needed for public education, libraries, and transportation. This is sometimes referred to as "crowding out." The pressure to fill one pot of money, without expanding the revenue stream, means other pots get short shrift.

Ms. Raimondo held a hundred or so town hall meetings in a teeny state like Rhode Island, talking to individuals and showing what the future would be if things were not changed. It wasn't a pretty picture. She worked hard and ultimately was able to make changes to the pension system because of the widespread public support that she was given. Of course, there have been court challenges to her work. She was a Democrat, but she inspired me. She didn't quit—even though she faced really tough odds. And she didn't quit because to her it was hugely important. Libraries, schools, buses, lots of activities funded by tax dollars were potentially on the chopping block. My father would have liked her and probably would have said admiringly, "She's as tough as an old boot!" She obviously was successful since she is now the governor of the state.

Gina Raimondo's goal was state finances; mine was more intrusive in a way. Texas is a very large state, and visiting with voters by going door-to-door wasn't going to be possible; so in 2012 I set out on my own set of town hall meetings. I held about forty of them across the state, where I talked about the financial information citizens were able to get from state taxing entities such as counties, cities, and schools.

What I saw was both sad and eye opening. Men and women all over the state complained that they couldn't get hard numbers from their school boards, superintendents, city halls, mayors, county judges, or others in charge of public entities—and they were frustrated. They tried open-records requests, which is usually an efficient way to get public records if you are a citizen. Texas actually has a good open records statute and generally a request for information has to be delivered in ten days, barring certain exceptions.

One of the last things I did as a state rep in the Texas House was to get a bill passed that required the state attorney general to respond to opinion requests about an open-records request within 180 days. *The Dallas Morning News* had been waiting two years for a response such as this. Governments were refusing to comply by using delays—and I thought that was just flat wrong. I didn't get the bill passed in the usual way on the floor as an independent bill. Instead, I turned it into an amendment after it passed through a committee. Sylvester Turner, now the mayor of Houston, added it on to his bill during a floor vote. Pretty nifty, huh? One door shut, and another one opened.

I was committed to government transparency. You might say I got rabid. The more I heard that ordinary people all across the state were being stiffed by bureaucrats, the madder I got. But I was really naïve. Once again, I thought good ideas should be winners. If Gina Raimondo had done it in a very tough environment, it should be easy here. Nope.

In the fall of 2012, I had a two bills drafted. (SB/HB 13 related to pension reform and SB/HB 14 related to increased government transparency.) I had done the appropriate things: contacted the leadership offices, got support (which is what the low bill numbers indicate since the lieutenant governor and the speaker reserve bill numbers under the number twenty for important legislation), found strong bill sponsors, and settled down to work. I figured I had a good plan, never dreaming everyone and his dog would try to kill it.

Pension woes out of Houston gave a boost to the first bill. As for the other bill aimed at financial transparency across all government entities—telling the truth about what you owe as a citizen, how you pay the debt, what things cost, basic kitchen table stuff—it all seemed very straightforward. But the legislative session of 2013 turned out to be excruciating.

I was told repeatedly that the transparency bill was a hard bill. "Why?" I asked.

"No one wants to vote on it."

"What? Why not?"

The Internet is the new public square and it is the only real way for an ordinary person to get access to information.

We had all campaigned on telling the truth, being fiscally conservative, and so on. I used the phrase ad nauseam "It's Their Money." I meant it was the taxpayer's money. I meant it then and mean it today. Superintendents, mayors, county judges, lawyers working for water districts that collected money, mayors—you name it—they all came unglued.

The bill asked these units of government to *please, pretty please,* tell the public about what they owed by—shocker—putting their debt information on the Internet. Oh, no. Too expensive. I knew it was a sham. I testified in a public hearing that by using Facebook I could set up a fake city, put the entire budget of the state of Texas on it, for no cost—except paying for the time it took someone to do it. The Internet is the new public square and it is the only real way for an ordinary person to get access to information.

Costs of school construction, for example. In a hearing, I was told that the average person would never be able to understand any of it. When I pointed out that homeowners routinely made huge decisions for their personal finances in buying homes, and getting a mortgage, I was told, "That isn't the same thing."

My opponents thought we were too dumb to know but smart enough to pay. I got pretty peeved. Just like I did with the Rio Grande Electric Co-op power line. Even if the government told taxpayers about where their money went, they would be too "dumb" to understand it!

The session dragged on, but by April it was clear the opposition was winning. County judges roared that they couldn't afford it, yet the smallest county in Texas by population, Loving County, had a website. Obviously the judges in large urban counties were fudging.

So were mayors. One told me to my face that the voters would be upset if they knew that they already were on the hook for over a billion dollars. I said to him, "It's their money. They're entitled." I didn't make the sale.

There was no way in hell I was going to quit.

What else did I do? Remember, if one door starts to shut, get your boots on and kick another one open. The day after the session adjourned, and the transparency bill failed, I had my agency launch a new website: www.TelltheTruthTexas.org. And we pledged that we would put virtually all of the information in the transparency bill on the website for everyone to see. Everyone—free of charge. There was no way in hell I was going to quit.

That took us about fifteen months.

When I would get discouraged, I remembered a saying my father used. "*Non Illegitimi Carborundum.*" Basically a fake Latin phrase for "Don't let the bastards grind you down." He had a wooden figurine in the ranch office, sitting on top of the filing cabinets, with the words in it. I had asked him what it meant and he told me. Those were obviously words he lived by—keep going, don't quit, and don't get ground down. I don't know which bastard he might have been thinking about, but I was seeing a whole bunch of folks waiting to grind my effort down.

It seems to me that the opposition to open access to information runs across a wide variety of spectrums, but that it is most dangerous when it comes to public dollars paid by taxpayers.

We had been issuing reports analyzing school districts on the relationship between how they spent money and their academic performance. It was called the Financial Allocation Study of Texas (FAST) and had already made some school superintendents very angry. We showed that certain schools achieved stellar academic performance while spending very little as a result of efficiencies; other schools did the opposite. I suspect this information, which was freely available and on the Internet, caused enough heartburn to convince schools they didn't need or want any more information. To this day, some of them are still convinced I have it in for them. Sometimes it's just too hard to bridge the gap between their self-interest and that of the public, and you just have to keep moving ahead.

The school construction data fight in the legislature had gotten my dander up, and we decided to use another weapon in the arsenal. We sent open records requests to the 1,000-plus Texas school districts, requesting information from them on the number of square feet, cost per square foot, cost per student, and expected student population for every single instructional building that had been built since 2007. Our state's open records law required a response within ten days, unless the information was probably confidential or there was a considerable difficulty in obtaining it. The schools had the information since they had written the contracts and paid the bills. However, the information seemed to be elusive. In some instances, obtaining it took way beyond the statutory ten days. And in some cases it took as much as one hundred days, but we persevered. How did we get it? We sent follow-up emails, made calls—repeatedly—and finally told a few dilatory districts we were going to publicize the fact that they refused to comply. I am reliably informed that they are still angry with our report, believing it to be inaccurate. Since the only information we had was from them, I am at a loss to understand the inaccuracies.

That information is still on the comptroller's website as an archived report. We saw that schools varied widely in cost per square foot. Some used architectural templates to keep costs down, others had to deal with hurricane issues, others just liked fancy buildings. But at least the paying public could be involved and have input based on facts.

But here is the follow-up. While I was in office, we felt this information was important. I have been out of office since January of 2015. I learned last spring that my successor did not feel his office should continue to provide the information about school performance and efficiency and the legislature wasn't going to fund it through another agency. I was taken by surprise since I hadn't been given a hint. Not have this information? How else could a parent, employer, anyone, ever get good information about how well a school both delivered education and managed the taxpayer resources? We also knew some schools wouldn't want the analysis.

I called the professor at Texas A&M University who had done much of the original work on FAST. I asked her if she wanted it to continue, and she said yes. She and I worked with the University of Texas at Dallas and were able to persuade the state Commissioner of Education that I would pay for a continued effort to provide school efficiency data, using leftover campaign funds, if he would assist in getting us the permission. Before leaving public office, I had set up a separate effort, Texans for Positive Economic Policy, to bring non-political information to all Texans, and a website at www.lonestarsuccess.com. This seemed a perfect fit. He agreed and we launched a revised program on May 25, 2016, named Texas Smart Schools.

The session of 2013 showed how the legislature didn't want transparency, and the subsequent one, of 2015, showed how easy it is to kill a good program if you don't want it. Except—like the night of the living dead, I keep coming back.

My husband asked me right after the session ended in 2013 what I needed to do that would take five and a half years to do (he assumed I would run for reelection in 2014 and have a new four-year term) instead of the remaining eighteen months in my existing term of office. I thought about it. Actually, there was nothing. I told him I could do it all in the time remaining. He said that he didn't want to wait any longer for us to have more time together. I had seen some doors shut, some open, but in every case, I felt the goal was too important to call it quits. Maybe there were other ways I could continue to fight on.

Every one of us has things we want to do. Be the best parent, be the best daughter, accomplish some long-held goal, make our community better. Whatever our destiny is, we can do it—by not quitting and by being flexible. And we and only we can truly drive our own destiny—no one else can.

We wrapped up all of our projects, delivered what we had promised, and I left.

Making that choice was important. I had chosen to get on and off a career escalator before. Once again, I was deciding to do something different. I would do the things I really cared about.

But the fights wouldn't end. I would be freer than any time before to say what I thought, write as I think, and be bold in a new and different way. Very liberating.

* * *

Misty Copeland in her wonderful Under Armour commercials shows that she succeeded against nearly overwhelming odds, and the tagline of the commercial is "I will what I want." She never quit working to achieve her goals.

As I am writing this, I have been out of office for a year and a half and do I ever feel great. I am focusing on the topics and issues I care deeply about. I will what I want.

We women need to give ourselves the power—the power of positive, optimistic thinking. And the power of saying "I will not give in. I will not let the forces against me succeed. I will propel myself across the finish line."

Politics was a rough sport. I absorbed a few punches, but it was fiercely rewarding. We have to enter the game. We have to want to win. Life itself can deliver a series of punches. Resilience is the key to our survival. And self-confidence is the necessary companion to that resilience. How many times have you heard a man say, "I'm sorry" as he begins a sentence or asks a question, as we women so often do? Where is our self-confidence?

A radio program on NPR on September 8, 2015, exposed the differences between women and men in applying for Kickstarter funding. Two researchers, one from the University of North Carolina and one from the University of Pennsylvania Wharton School, looked at 90,000 start-up projects. They took a look at the difference, if any, between optimism and overconfidence. Essentially, the guys were more confident, even when their first attempts failed. The word "arrogant" was used to describe their attitudes. They just kept trying. They didn't quit. If the woman didn't succeed on her first try, she thought she had a bad idea and didn't try again. She was trying to be rational. The guys kept trying, throwing the spaghetti on the wall, and eventually something stuck. Even when the women were funded the first time, they put it down to luck. The men took it as a sign of their brilliance.

It wasn't luck. It was their brains, and talent, for both women and men. The takeaway for me is that we need to build a culture where women feel more willing to try—to take the risk. Some of that risk is in how we present ourselves. Being relentlessly positive may be seen as being overly aggressive, when it is simply persistence rearing its beautiful head. Men seem to take risks more easily—maybe because they feel they deserve a certain outcome. But we need to change culture so that women feel the same way. That is part of the purpose behind Herdacity.

When you succeed, you are a winner.
In some cases, you are a hero.

Women can definitely boost the morale of other women, and I hope we will all embrace this behavior. I suspect many of us might not feel able to fight back for ourselves, but we are more than willing to fight to help a friend. And once we have successfully helped a friend, we have learned how—and we can then apply those tactics to our own lives in the future.

We need to see ourselves as winners—because we are.

There were definitely times in my life when I wasn't sure if I could do something. But I took one tiny step forward, then another, then another. I imagine it is common for everyone, men and women, to wonder if they are up to taking on a new task. When you succeed, you are a winner. In some cases, you are a hero.

Go to Google and look up Charlotte Heffelmire and what she did in January of 2016. Her father was working on a truck in the garage, when the jack collapsed and the truck fell on him. Gasoline spilled and the garage caught on fire. The daughter, at 5'6" and 120 pounds, lifted the truck off him, drove the truck out of the garage, and saved the family. Would she have ever, in her wildest moments, thought she could have done something like that? No. But she did. Unfortunately, she had to give up her plans to go to the Air Force Academy where she had been admitted, because of the injury to her back. But she is now looking at public service.

You can bet her father was hoping she wouldn't be a quitter and she wasn't. Each of us can find something we care enough about that gives us the unexpected energy and courage to go way past where we thought we could go. That is part of my challenge to you. Decide to direct your destiny. Be the architect and implementer of your own plan, your life's path.

In my own case, I have been able to find things I cared deeply about—children, working to keep the ranch going, helping the public. Once I was in motion, I just kept on moving. I didn't set out to do any of these things in the beginning, but each step forward made its own kind of sense. Things will pop up to impede your momentum. Newton's law of physics basically says once a stationary object starts to move, it will continue to move at a constant speed until it hits another object. My view is if there is an object ahead, get rid of it! The bastards weren't going to get me down and the word "quitter" was one I never wanted applied to me.

Now it's just a question of what to do next. But I think I have that figured out, too.

CHAPTER 11

Lessons Learned

L eaving public office has given me the chance to have a breather while I think about what I want to do—what I enjoy doing—and what I really *have* to do to feel most alive, energized, and valuable. My next steps are still not fully defined, but I hope they reflect a bold vision and require me to show courage.

When I was in my mid-forties and launched into a political career of uncertain duration or effect, I wanted to change things I didn't like. I was motivated by a passion to do, to engage, to modify, and the belief that I had to be proud of what I did when I was finished.

But not everyone wants to be an activist. And it certainly isn't for everyone. Although I am still working on various projects, retiring from public service has allowed me to develop a rather different lens for what I want to do with my time.

So be deliberate about taking care of yourself—
mentally, physically, and emotionally.
Carve out that special place. Don't wait.

And using the word "time" as a measuring stick is increasingly important, as I get older. Many of us have experienced or will experience the loss of a parent, or a loved one, or a friend. Recently, in the material from Vassar about our upcoming reunion in 2016, I received a list of deceased college classmates, and was astonished to see that a few had died in their late twenties or thirties. Not their seventies. Not their forties. Way too young. And I don't know if they had the time or ability to carve out a special space for themselves. So be deliberate about taking care of yourself—mentally, physically, and emotionally. Carve out that special place. Don't wait.

The ranch is that place for me. I remember life on the ranch and how water was vital. If the wind blew, and the pipes in the ground didn't have holes, and the leathers worked, we could pull water up from under the ground, and it would fill a tank. From there it would flow into a series of troughs connected by pipelines. Often a windmill was near a tree, and as the metal vanes of the windmill turned, I would hear two sounds I love: leaves rustling and the drip or slow flow of water into a tank, particularly a metal tank in the days before plastic. For me, being outdoors has always been hugely important.

Even today, if I can't be outside every few days, sitting, thinking, writing, or reading, I can detect a distinct darkening mood. Music always helps dispel that mood for me. I tell myself, "Get up, go turn on the music, do something!"

Doing something to create happiness is imperative. I try each day to choose happiness. Sometimes it can feel easier to sit and let events overtake us. But even though it is harder to do, it is so much more valuable to be intentional about our lives and our paths.

That kind of intentionality can come in all sorts of arenas as we direct our paths. I have met people through Rotary who devote a considerable amount of their time and energy to helping others in very specific and local projects. We must take the time to look around so we can match our interests with local community needs. These volunteers are directing their time to help others. You may want to take a different route.

I don't want to lean in all the time. I want to lean back, or step sideways, but wherever I take a step, I make sure it is intentional. That way I am controlling—to the extent I can—my own destiny. That's not to say that the unexpected can't happen. Murphy's Law is just as likely to strike as not!

At various times in our lives, different messages from both within ourselves and from others can call out to us. What we do about those messages is up to us. Just be open to them—from whatever direction and whatever source they might come. Whether from TV, a friend's idle comment, an article you read online, or a friend's personal story—be open to the messages. Women of all ages, life experiences, and backgrounds suddenly step off the fast track and onto creative pathways. Yours might be sculpture, a renewed interest in art, or writing. Once we see the path and put our feet on it, we are in control.

* * *

Remember when you were a kid and you had so much energy you just had to run, and gallop, and leap? I was a skinny, long-legged kid and I leapt for the sheer joy of it. Sometimes I was a pony, other times I was a princess with long flowing hair, galloping through the wild countryside. My hair was a scarf secured with three wavy bobby pins and it flowed magically. Children all over the world leap and play happily until adults tell them not to. Yes—until they are told not to. And girls get those messages more frequently and earlier than boys. So, absolutely leap and play in your life! Why not? Who cares if others are watching and judging? It's your life. Make it what you want it to be. I believe that the freedom to feel unrestricted enough to play and leap is the most important gift you can give a child. Do the same for yourself. You have no limits. Own your happiness.

In my years of leaping and running and pushing or kicking doors open, I have always tried to feel joy. With age have come different techniques, but the goal is the same. We are on our life's path and we don't know, when we start, exactly where it will end.

What seems most important is that each one of us must have a real and clear sense of who we are, what we are, and where we want to be. If we know this, then we can figure out how to get there.

*   *   *

If we want to help others, especially other women, we must be clearly attuned to what they want. We must ask ourselves if can we help them in a way different from what we may have assumed. We need to understand their goals, their dreams.

It was because of my change in perspectives about the status of women in the spring of 2015, based on the Austin City Council snafu, that I launched The Anywhere Woman Project (a 501(c)(4) nonpolitical education project) a couple of months later—which holds that a woman's place is anywhere she wants it to be. Let me repeat: anywhere *she* wants it to be. We gave the organization a shorter name, which really captures the power of all women: Herdacity—shorthand for "her audacity."

What is Herdacity? It's a place where women dare . . . to do whatever they want to do, to achieve the destiny that suits them. Daring can sometimes be in short supply, and this is where we hope to provide an online meeting place for women where they can connect with each other, share experiences and stories, and both give and receive advice, empowerment, and encouragement. Where they can be free to dare to express themselves, dare to dream, even dare to disappoint others if necessary.

We should always ask ourselves whether there is anyone we owe more to than we owe to ourselves. In a very real sense, we owe it to ourselves to be the person we want to be, to direct our lives toward the areas where we want to participate. While it may sound simple, doing that can take real courage.

We have to not let ourselves be held back by inchoate fears. One of the best ways I can think of to remove those fears is to connect with someone else—someone who can help talk us down or talk us up. Connectivity, in my experience, is a particularly powerful tool and often not utilized enough. Everyone talks a lot about wanting to communicate, but sometimes it can be hard to find someone to connect with. We hope Herdacity can be that place. Our website—**www.herdacity.org**—has areas we call "campfires" set up to give women a place to express themselves freely when they are discussing topics that interest them.

> *Each of us possesses some secret skill,*
> *some strength, some trait that we may not*
> *even recognize, that can help us achieve our*
> *dreams and focus on our aspirations.*

We want to help women in whatever endeavor they choose. I have been fortunate—fortunate to be born into a family with two loving parents, fortunate to be tall and always visible, fortunate to have strong roots in the land. Other women have their own fortunes—the parts of them that make them unique and powerful. Some have the most extraordinarily compelling personalities. Some exude a miraculous calm, which helps those around them. Some have a vital electricity that sparks enthusiasm in others. Each of us possesses some secret skill, some strength, some trait that we may not even recognize, that can help us achieve our dreams and focus on our aspirations. We need to know our dreams deep down and hold them close, in case others try to talk us out of them.

*   *   *

I want to challenge this notion about women's supposed lack of confidence. Yes, women are different from men—in many ways—but why should that define what we think we can achieve, or whether or not we have a voice in a matter or a place at the table, wherever that table is? I recall the words of Marian Wright Edelman, president and founder of the Children's Defense Fund, who said, "You can't be what you can't see." Whom have you "seen" and who inspires you to be who you want to be?

As a girl, I heard about Amelia Earhart. Because my mother liked golf, I had heard of the famous golfer Babe Didrikson Zaharias, who was a superb athlete in a number of sports. Madame Curie and a few other female names were all I heard about as role models when I was growing up. Isn't that amazing? Through thousands of years, our textbooks and histories had just a few women—certainly stellar, but of course those women never adequately represented all the women who have done so much. That lack of visibility of accomplished women, that striking absence of the camera focusing on them, has to change—in schools and higher education, magazines, books, TV, and the media. When women make up over 50 percent of the population and yet have such poor exposure, something is clearly out of whack.

So, which women inspire the young women of today? Where are the role models who tell them "Yes, you can do it"? The inspiring story of the ballerina Misty Copeland struck a chord in girls across the globe, not just because she is African-American in a largely white ballet world, but because of her extraordinary persistence against nearly insuperable odds. Her memoir showed incredible struggles that turned into triumphs. She had remarkable tenacity, grit, and talent. But most of all, she drew courage from a place she knew, absolutely knew, that told her she could "do it"—"it" meaning ballet. Taylor Swift, Katy Perry, Emma Watson, and a host of other highly visible personalities have been able to capture our imagination in the entertainment industry. I would suspect that each of them at some point had to boost their self-confidence. But they also knew and believed in some deep sense they had to persevere.

I have known extraordinarily successful women who defined success on their own terms in all sorts of arenas: churches, volunteer service, running major enterprises, succeeding in so-called men's areas, and so forth. They aimed for it and achieved it. It is my hope that each of us is able to define what success means for us, and also help those around us achieve their goals. While I am focused on women in this project, part of my reason for doing so comes from observing my own family.

I wanted my three sons to achieve what they wanted so *they* would be happy on their own terms. It isn't always easy for us mothers to actually let this happen. I had this fact brought home to me by my youngest son. I had established a fairly busy (you could say hectic) schedule for him, believing that he "needed" numerous activities. One day, as we were driving home from school, he asked if he could just stop all of his after-school activities. I asked him why.

He said, "I want to be able to sit outside in the magnolia tree in our yard." He had such a clear vision of how he wanted to spend his time and it most definitely wasn't rushing around. I am still amazed that he articulated it, and very grateful. I was so focused on cramming this kid into the box I had crafted that I hadn't looked at the box or my son . . . did they even match? What was it I was trying to do and why? He was on his journey, and his clear view of where he wanted to go—at least for the next year—was sobering. I had been running over him with the mommy wagon and he wanted out from under it.

But if we're lucky, our children sometimes can and do find a way to let us know what they need for themselves and from us. We should listen and learn.

We stopped his activities immediately. I was just glad he was able to articulate what he needed. And I also remembered those lazy summer afternoons when I had sat in a tree in the big yard next to me, thinking, listening, being. I needed that and he clearly did too. It isn't always so simple for our children to buck the path their parents put forward. But if we're lucky, our children sometimes can and do find a way to let us know what they need for themselves and from us. We should listen and learn.

Each of us needs to be heard in some basic, real sense. Children need to be heard by their parents so that we can help them be happier. We need to be heard by ourselves as well, and we need to listen to that little mental itch that says we are on a wrong path, somehow, some way. How many times have you thought that something you were doing wasn't fulfilling, interesting, or was too time-consuming? Perhaps you kept overcommitting yourself, but didn't want to deal with the matter and the potential fallout? In my own case, too many times I just sat there and stewed until the pressure built up to where I had to pay attention and change my own path. Sometimes it took nerve that I didn't think I could muster. The situation with my first husband was a classic case of my fear of social pressures nearly wrecking my life. I wish I'd had a place where I could have communicated anonymously with others. But first, I also had to recognize that I had a real problem that needed fixing.

Since it is absolutely true that life will throw curveballs our way, we all do learn, somehow, to deal with them. When often, we didn't think we could. We lose jobs, spouses, economic security, friendships. Our health changes, a myriad of things can hit us. The miraculous thing is that we virtually always end up coping. We deal with the adversity, the shift in our life view. Women are tremendously resilient, skilled at coping.

When life hands us a bushel of lemons, of course we make lemonade, but we also make lemon pies, lemon cakes, lemon quiches, you name it. We have always found ways to direct our destiny around a problem.

* * *

Offering to help someone else can be a turning point for that individual and have unexpected and far-reaching consequences. And when you have done something for someone else, it makes you feel like a million dollars! I have become a big fan of people who "connect" people, because there is a lot of power and opportunity inherent in connecting with others.

I met Bob Campbell about a year ago at a downtown lunch event in Austin. Our paths had crossed earlier, but this lunch event cemented our relationship. Bob had been with a major consulting firm, which reached across many spheres—management, global relations, trade, and so forth.

I told him that I was working on the issues facing women today and he immediately expressed an interest. Even more than that, he took an active hand in helping me find women who might be interested in the same topic.

He performed this task very simply. I would get an email from Bob addressed to Susan (me) and someone else. He introduced us online and then left it up to us to generate a meeting. It worked like a charm. So far, he has introduced me to ten or so people, each of whom I have later met in person. In turn, many of these encounters have produced other contacts in fields of interest or endeavors where I previously didn't have any contacts or particular insight.

This kind of connectivity is very powerful because it's real. It isn't a phone call; it's in person and in a place where both parties want to meet. We each get something out the meeting. And that "getting" might lead us to a new view, a different perspective, or a whole new way to analyze a particular problem. This connectivity doesn't really fit into the mentorship or sponsorship category, because it seems more general, more wide open. That also makes it very interesting because it allows for a weird kind of spontaneity. What on earth am I going to learn? Will I pursue a further meeting? And the always-important question—am I, in my turn, providing something of value to the other person?

These rather random meetings can produce some really big consequences. Another friend, Paul Carrozza here in Austin, also excels at connecting people to make his community a better place. For example, I would get a phone call or a text with a random request asking whether I could I meet with someone to just chat. Because of this, I met people involved in car racing, which led me to play a major role in bringing the US Grand Prix to Austin. I met a basketball coach who helped me shape my ideas on children's fitness and others who were thinking and doing interesting things. The totally different life views and experiences helped open my eyes, and I tried to help them achieve their goals. Paul and I have stayed in touch over the years—mostly on the topic of children's health. He was a tireless advocate when we were trying to get legislation to change school lunch foods. He is a running and fitness fanatic who has done a great deal for many people in Austin and across the country.

One group in particular is individuals who are more than one hundred pounds overweight. He has started them walking, jogging, and slowly running. He gave them a dream of moving their own bodies that they had never had, and the results in their mood, energy, and life views have been wonderful. He helped launch Marathon Kids, which gives children the confidence to believe that they can achieve fitness through running or walking. He has put his passion and energy into something that speaks to his deepest being. He truly does know when he is doing what he wants, and it makes him happy. He has continually dared to be the man and influencer he wants to be. We can all take a lesson from him.

Lisa Woods also makes a habit out of this kind of connecting. She is able—in a seemingly effortless way—to bridge the gaps between people. Her model is always positive. She delivers help and connects people in ways that enhance everyone in the personal equation. That is a really miraculous talent. First, of course, she has helped me over the years. But she is often called on to help turn a nonprofit or academic department around. Her skills are rooted in being both wonky and personal—she gets the data together and then helps build coalitions to achieve the goal of the organization based on hard facts. In my experience, that is a rare talent. Oftentimes the wonky people aren't able to inspire. She can do both. She has friends on both coasts, and in Texas and Colorado, and is always looking for ways to get people together to make their own lives better.

Bob, Paul, and Lisa have taught me that you have to be proactive if you want to accomplish your goals. It would be fabulous if the dream job, dream opportunity, or dream relationship just dropped into your lap, but generally something else drops out of the sky and it isn't pretty! So you have to take your future and your happiness into your own hands. You have to direct your own destiny.

What does that really mean? It means you have to be both daring and measured, a risk taker and a hard-eyed analyst, a dreamer and a pragmatist. Let's just assume for the moment that you do know exactly what you want, and where you want to be. Congratulations. You are in the lucky minuscule percentage of people so in tune with themselves and their skills, ambitions, and desires that they have it all mapped out.

While each thing I did was intentional (going to law school, running for office), I didn't have a thirty-year game plan. In that sense, looking backward, the path was never clear showing me that I would arrive at the place where I am today. But each step also made sense. In addition, I had a No-Sour-Grapes rule.

I didn't want to look back, years further down the road, and find I had failed to do something that I would regret years later. That simple rule helped move me forward, rather than stand still. Each time I changed direction, I had a deliberate, even if not decades-long view of the next project, the next goal. I have done some really fun things in my life, and I still don't have any sour grapes about missing something. My bucket list isn't about places to go, it is about things to get done. The best thing about these changes in paths is that each career or life change helped me hugely. I grew from them and I took risks. The risks produced successes and gave me the confidence to continue taking more risks. The horizon of my thinking expanded way out from where it had been and I saw things more clearly.

I saw that I could achieve beyond my parents' goals for me. I could do things I had never imagined doing. And I kept moving, because the steps were big but ultimately doable. Each one of us knows just how much to risk, and what skills and intellectual assets we bring to bear if we don't let fear get in our way. I have had my own fears. Some resolved over time, and some I just had to kick in the teeth. Putting up with a bit of fear has enabled me to move forward farther and faster than I would have thought possible—and it can for you, too.

Abandoning fear is freedom. Irrational fears can be debilitating. Sometimes they can also be very instructive. One night I had such an experience.

Back when the kids were in school, I would often leave them with my husband while I went out to the ranch by myself for three or four days.

Because the ranch was so isolated, I always slept with a shotgun on the bed next to me, to make me feel safe. We did have occasional break-ins, but normally we weren't home when the intruders showed up. Occasionally, however, someone would just suddenly appear out of nowhere. They would have been lying on the ground waiting to see who was at the house. Generally, they were people coming from Mexico or Central America who wanted food. If they did break in, there was usually no damage, just a few missing cans or a pair of boots or shoes.

That night in particular, I jerked awake after midnight, my heart pounding so loudly I thought whoever was there could hear it. I heard feet—wearing boots—outside my bedroom door. I was absolutely positive someone was right outside.

I grabbed the shotgun and bolted out of bed, then tiptoed over to sit in the chair against the window—facing the door to the room with the gun across my lap. I was trying to be ready to defend myself. Where was my dog? Why hadn't she barked? She must have been killed. She would have barked. I knew she would. They ("they" are always monstrous, menacing, and much better at fighting than we are) were outside my door. Silent.

Wait. Still silent? I knew I had heard their boots. I knew it. He or they were going to come at me through the other door through the bathroom that connected to a second bedroom. I breathed lightly and shallowly. I had read about forward soldiers in combat called LRP (long range patrol) who slid silently through the jungle, invisible and unheard. This had to be one of those guys.

Really? In the Big Bend about a kazillion miles from anywhere? Admittedly, my fear didn't seem rational, but I couldn't talk myself out of it.

What was I going to do? Sit bolt upright all night? Go out and face a nightmare? Not yet. The chair was very hard. My back was starting to hurt. I was breathing high and shallow. I hadn't yet hyperventilated, but I knew that was a risk. And of course—no paper sack anywhere to breathe into.

After twenty minutes of this silent and potentially deadly stand-off, with no dog barking, I quietly pushed the bedroom door open. Nothing. Nobody. The house seemed empty. I kept swiveling my head looking in the dark corners of the living room, then the dining room. I carried the shotgun ready to inflict serious bodily injury, one hand with the finger in the trigger guard, and the other supporting the barrel, pointing forward. Where *was* my dog? There she was. Just fine and sleeping happily right outside the kitchen door on the stoop outside. I didn't open the door. Still worried, I flipped the switch inside the house to light up the porch, and I could see her through the upper glass half of the window.

So where was the deadly menace? The next morning, in the calm light of day, I saw a dark stain on the ceiling in the dining room. A ringtail or some other kind of animal had undoubtedly been roaming around in the attic over my bed, causing sound transference through the attic rafters that sounded like booted feet. A four-footed, wily rodent was my silent and deadly monster.

Lesson learned: I wasn't going to let myself ever be this frightened again, and I haven't.

*   *   *

When I got into politics, I worried I wouldn't do the right thing. Would I be swayed by a group of powerful people I would be too afraid to buck?

I work hard, do my best to be thoughtful, and try to make good decisions. Invariably, they are not always one hundred percent correct— but I do my best. I have a particular metric that I use to give me strength and confidence.

When I got into politics, I worried I wouldn't do the right thing. Would I be swayed by a group of powerful people I would be too afraid to buck? Would I fail to listen to my intellect and get sucked into a power play? Would I be afraid to stand up for what I thought was right? Would I have the grit I needed to stay true to who I was? So I thought about it and I adopted a 3:00 a.m. test. If I wake up at 3:00 a.m. and feel I have done something wrong, then I have.

Once, I said something about a public figure I liked, but I used really terrible phrasing and it made the newspapers. I wrote a letter apologizing to the individual, but you can't ever really take back what you've said. The stupidity of my behavior has stuck with me. It is never good enough to apologize when you should have done the right thing up front.

In the world of politics, Reggie Bashur is one person who stood out. He was someone who always wanted to do the right thing. I worked with him for at least ten years, and he was one of the most extraordinary friends I've ever had. He died a couple of years ago after a short illness. What made him stand out was that he always wanted the best for me—not for him, not for someone else. He helped me run and win two elections as state comptroller, but he told me repeatedly that I had to do what I wanted to do—not what someone else wanted. He was telling me to direct my destiny, even against opposing tides. He was a big dark-haired bear of a guy, with Lebanese ancestry, and I do not know how to replace his intelligence, thoughtfulness, and warmth.

But when you have strayed off your path and receive a bad kind of wake-up call, you know that it will be far better to do the right thing up front than worry about cleaning up the mess behind the circus animal later. Easier on both the shovel and your back—and certainly on your friends. When I occasionally wake up now at 3:00 a.m., it is because my brain has been processing all that I have to do, and I know I need to get a head start on it. Sometimes, however, it is because I am a perpetual worrier. I could lie in bed panicking over something, but by just getting up and going to sit in the living room, solutions emerge from the fog of fear. I don't know if it will work for you, but literally being upright gives me strength to figure out what is bugging me, ponder on a solution, and then start to work on it. So far, it has always worked. Once I decide how to fix it, I do.

We have to engage ourselves in order to be strong. And we have to keep moving—physically and mentally. Continuing to move forward requires us to believe we can do it, and should do it. And how can we give ourselves the confidence to do what we need to do? First, I think you learn bit by bit, just like driving a car. I know I scared my father as I was learning to drive. I hit curbs, missed visual cues. But little by little, I learned to pay attention in multiple directions. I became a much better driver.

So too with flying. I learned to look on three axes, for airplanes above, below and beside, or in front. My brain was trained to process information, and that gave me the confidence to take off and land. Skiing was the same thing. My point is that we can train ourselves to become capable of new tasks, and that success then gives us the confidence to perform other new tasks.

Every time I started a new project or was in a new job or a new environment I had to say to myself, "If you can't do it today, you can do it tomorrow." Read, study, think. Absorb everything you can about the new environment. Don't be afraid. Be careful, and train yourself instead.

Get comfortable with yourself. Get comfortable with what you look like, how you think, speak, talk. Nobody can make you over but you. I've had my makeup done at the makeup counter like most of us have, and there is no way I can ever replicate how it's done by a professional. I just have to be comfortable doing it myself.

Try something new. It always leads to confidence. Imagine yourself doing some new activity. I am a big klutz when it comes to electronic equipment, but I am trying to teach myself to master new things in that realm. I know that just by making the effort, I will give myself confidence, because I will have learned something new. That tells me I can learn the next new thing, and the next, and the one after that. We humans respond to both internal and external stimuli, and the glow of success from accomplishing something new is a great stimulus.

And last, but definitely not least, tell yourself, "You are worth it." Don't be afraid to stand for and stand up for yourself—you are the one in control.

Lt. General Michelle Johnson entered the Air Force Academy in the class of 1981, the second coed class. In an article that appeared on FoxNews.com on July 2, 2015, she writes crisply and lucidly about her career, but undoubtedly omitted many of the struggles that she faced. Today she is the Superintendent of the US Air Force Academy, and has the power to change the culture.

Did she have to endure some hazing during her time there as a student? Of course. Did she complain about it? I suspect not, but rather she decided she would do something about it when she could. Did things need to change? Absolutely. She writes, and in so doing implicitly recognizes that change for the good has occurred: "The climate is more inclusive, the culture more respectful. Antagonistic relationships are no longer tolerated."

There is quite a bit contained in those two sentences. She indicates clearly that an older culture needed to change and that it did.

So how do we object to stupidity without seeming fragile or whiny? How can we argue without being called bitches, cats, or something else? Before I got my driver's license, my father would drop me off at a nearby movie theater to see a new release. In the olden days, there were sometimes intermissions—a break in the movie when you could get more candy, refill your coke, or stretch your legs. One particular time, I went outside the theater during the intermission and a group of three or four boys came out as well. I must have been about thirteen and was 5'10". They came over to me. One looked up and asked, "How's the weather up there?"

I looked down at them, and with absolutely no forethought, said, "It's raining," and made spitting noises. They trotted away quickly. I don't regret it. They needed better manners—as did I.

It seems that we are always going to encounter situations where we don't feel comfortable with how we are treated. But the requirement for good behavior runs both ways—from us to other women, and from other people to us.

I watched the Emma Watson speech at the United Nations on the HeForShe effort, and several things stood out for me. She discussed gender equality, and she discussed words and adjectives that are strong and can express strength. No stereotype defines the real you, but in referring to the use of the word feminism, she pointed out that it was "awkward" for some.

She said she was lucky because she had loving parents who made her feel she could do things. She also talked about male and female stereotypes that say men have to be strong and women have to be feminine and the weaker sex. She was making the point that the stereotyping she deplored is pervasive.

That certainly struck home for me. I told our three sons that it was always fine to cry. My father (the very tough rancher) and I would both choke up watching certain movies, or thinking about events. One in particular involved a cousin. My father very much loved his first cousin David McGehee, who died in his late twenties before the discovery of penicillin. My father would tear up as he talked about how much he missed his cousin. I believe the ability to show emotion is manly. It makes men better. And conversely, women are better when they can embrace the concept of being strong, self-reliant, and decisive.

Since I am decades older than Ms. Watson, my perspective of what constitutes "equal" may be different. We should, of course, have equal pay for equal work and for equal experience. The challenge I faced early in my career as a lawyer was that I wanted to stay home for a few months with my first two sons, but I was acutely aware of the risk. If I stayed out too long, I would risk sliding out of place in line in the Dallas District Attorney's office. I thought then and still think that it is fair that if you get off the career escalator, and experience counts for something, you are making a conscious decision to affect the forward motion of your future career.

When I had been at home with my second son a little over seven months, I got a call from my boss. I could return to work at some later date and start at the bottom of the ladder, or come back in two weeks and stay at my level. My husband and I discussed the pros and cons, and I went back to work.

Make no mistake. I know I was very lucky to be able to stay home for that long, and to be able to forgo a salary for the months I did. I don't regret any of it. For a mother, being able to stay home is something she will always cherish. My daughter-in-law was only able to stay home for three months from her job after the birth of her son. And it is impossible for many moms to be able to take more than the absolute minimum.

* * *

The time we take to help other people, whether family or friends, is one of the most important gifts we can give. Perhaps your church or religious community has a program to take meals to the elderly or shut-ins. The list is long for these opportunities. By helping others we are increasing our own worth as individuals and at the same time helping to illuminate a path for someone else. It may not be through advice. It may not be through work. It may simply be that by showing we care, we are making a bigger point.

I learned a lot from having that first puppy when I was twelve, because I had to learn to care for him. He couldn't communicate well, and I didn't have good dogspeak so had to receive visual cues and then figure them out. I have not had much luck with various cats over the years, but I hope and believe I have managed to learn to read my dogs.

This has helped me be the kind of person my dogs want me to be, and they know they can trust me (by and large) to provide a safe haven.

Having dogs has helped me with learning to read people. I probably could have used extra help when I think back to my grandmother, with her very disparate personas, and the fact I knew so little about her until she showed me more of her personality. I just didn't read her well. Listening is a very good way to learn about people.

When our friends are struggling with a decision in their lives, giving the gift of our time and our focused attention is enormously valuable to the recipient. Someone cares. Someone is listening. I can bounce ideas off of them and believe I will be heard.

Let me insert something here that I really find to be a big problem. We are supposedly paying attention to the person we are with, yet we are letting our phones or other devices interfere. As we try to help other women direct their destiny, we need to be in the now with them, in the present.

So Susan's rule for good behavior is turn off or silence your phones and smart watches. When someone you know is in need of help, be there, not out in the ether. And the second rule is don't consume all of the airtime or talking time yourself. Listen and you will learn more than you can by talking. When I used to talk to the men on the ranch about what had been going on in the last week or so, there were inevitably long pauses, punctuated by nearly silent sips from a coffee mug. The protocol to show respect was to just wait. Words would flow eventually. In our urban settings, the words will flow eventually and so will a smart decision. Let's wait for it.

CHAPTER 12

Make Your Own HERstory

Sally Bishop, a very smart English woman, was my roommate when I lived in New York in my early twenties. She is a gifted actress and director, and she and her husband are devoted to the theater. She has worked in human resources, run a catering company, done consulting for a car manufacturer, and is a talented serial entrepreneur. Nothing has ever held Sally back, as far as I can tell.

I was talking to her recently about the state of women. I told her about what we were trying to do with Herdacity and The Anywhere Woman Project. When I described the Austin City Council snafu, she started to laugh.

"Yes, it sounds exactly the same as over here."

We were both silent for a moment. How on earth could that be?

The United States, England, and numerous other countries seem to have moved forward very little in terms of respect for and appreciation of women in the last fifty years. Here are a few thoughts.

When those in high positions add negative comments into this atmosphere, it makes the uphill climb that much steeper. You may remember former Harvard President Larry Summers who made these types of comments in 2005. He basically said that there are relatively few women in top positions in science, perhaps due to "different availability of aptitude at the high end." A nice firestorm erupted after that, and he had to release the transcript and walk backward rather quickly. This then starts a whole series of stereotypes that perpetuate negativity directed at women and takes the focus off what the core issues are—and women everywhere hear this and internalize it. Genetically, they're different. Boys are better at all that kind of stuff, while girls don't have the necessary aptitude. And like the consultant in Austin, Summers used his young daughter to illustrate his views of women. To top it off, he dismissed the notion of bias against women in colleges and universities.

According to an article in *The Guardian*, Dr. Richard Freeman (who had invited Dr. Summers to speak) said the women "overreacted," and were "very sensitive." That is clearly a bad thing. Women should not be sensitive. In fact, even speaking about it is a bad thing. He compounded this by saying that "it does not seem insane to me that men and women, they have biological differences." Good grief. Back to Mars and Venus. And it is still going on ten years later.

Fast forward ten years to June of 2015, when a Nobel prize–winning physiologist in England suggested that women and men should have separate labs. Tim Hunt, a self-described male chauvinist, was speaking at the World Conference of Science Journalists in South Korea where he said the following: "Three things happen when they are in the lab: You fall in love with them, they fall in love with you, and when you criticize them they cry." Is this science, or bias?

Yes, Virginia, he did get in trouble. He resigned his position as honorary professor at University College London. One female professor from that college wrote on Twitter that she couldn't do any science work because she saw a photo of him and now she is in love. Pretty funny. Another English female scientist tweeted that she couldn't chair a morning meeting because she was too busy swooning and crying.

Most amusingly, when Tim Hunt tried to clean up his comments, he just made them worse. Naturally. My friend Sally had read all about him and she asked the same question I did—how on earth can this still be happening??

When I graduated from college in the late sixties, I understood in a very real way that there was a woman's place and a man's place, and they were quite different. But we were on the cusp of big societal change. Women's lib was just happening. Women were launching themselves in large numbers into areas that had seemed unattainable before. What was also apparent was that there were ways of shifting power if you tried to do it. But as far as role models in a variety of fields, there just weren't any in my textbooks.

Even at Vassar, there were no specific female role models. As I remember, female or male professors were not deemed stellar because of gender but rather each one stood on his or her merits. But because we were fortunate enough to go to a women's college right at the start of a supposed transformation of women's roles, we were excited. Things were going to change a lot.

Not so fast. When we hear even in 2016 about the continuing drop-off in interest in science and math among girls in middle school that has been going on for a very long time, we have to wonder why it is still happening. What messages are these young women receiving? Or rather, what messages are they not receiving? Are they being told they are wonderful at math? Or are they being discouraged?

And remember the geniuses on the staff of the Austin City Council in 2015? It seems not a whole lot has changed if tired tropes from the 1950s are being used to educate professionals in today's environment.

Once again, textbooks just don't have much to say about women, and textbooks are where young men and women learn about famous and/or significant people. A study in 2006 by Kay A. Chick from Penn State Altoona, published in *Social Studies Research and Practice*, looked at American history textbooks for kindergarten through high school and found that males were much more represented than women, and when women were mentioned, it was often done in sidebars, rather than in the main body of the page. (One statistic was very telling:

Reviews of eighteen high school textbooks on American history found that 1,335 women were mentioned, compared with 12,382 men.) This is actually better than earlier textbooks.

Why don't we see the names of famous women inventors, scientists, and the like in today's history books? As you might have guessed, women do not dominate the word game. Journalism is actually a male-dominated field. Men represent the majority of all supervisors, copy editors, reporters, writers, and photographers. A study by the American Society of News Editors showed that there is a two-to-one ratio in every category, except for photographers and videographers, where the disparity jumps to three to one.

As a kid, I was not going to be a super scientist. No such dreams. Airline stewardess—yes. Ballerina—until the reality of height reared its ugly head—yes. But why not a scientist? Because they just weren't talked about. Writers in whatever medium just didn't talk about women scientists. I saw stewardesses, but the notion of living my life in science never occurred to me. I had never seen a woman in science, except for our pediatrician; and she scared the hell out of me. The notion of women as inventors or world leaders in medicine wasn't on my radar. Let me repeat Marian Wright Edelman's comment: "You can't be what you can't see."

By way of illustration about my early lack of science chops, let me describe one failed effort. I had a project in sixth grade where I was supposed to make some kind of a map of Italy. We were to give it shape and definition using flour and water. I was supposed to make mountains.

It was not simple. Too much flour at first; then too much water; and then the mountains slumped. No self-respecting Caesar would have ever thought they were worth bothering about. The project was interesting, and having had real role models would have been very useful. So I am writing about women scientists because we need them, there aren't enough of them, and unfortunately we don't talk about them enough, which is why you've never heard of them. They were all amazing women and their stories need to be told.

If we women, starting from girlhood, aspire to lead, be self-confident, and have the gumption to do what we want in whatever arena we want, we need strong women to emulate. Women in science are a critical part of our past, although not a well-known part, and a vital part of our future. The unsung women in science have created new products, found solutions to big problems, and generally made the world a better place. I am going to give here a pretty random list of women who have invented everyday things you have heard of but were never informed that a woman invented them.

Patsy O. Sherman invented Scotchgard while she worked as a scientist at 3M. Very nifty, and I bet you didn't know about her. Evidently, it all started with an accident where some goop was dropped on the floor—and they couldn't clean it up. The fact that the substance was so hard to clean up sparked the notion that maybe it could be used as a way to protect fabrics. The spill on the floor was just the start of the invention process, but look where it took her. It was introduced to the public in 1956.

Mary Anderson invented windshield wipers in 1903 and received a patent for her work. What prompted this? She watched a streetcar driver try to drive in heavy, wet snow with poor visibility and wondered how to fix the problem.

Madam C. J. Walker invented hair products for African-American women and became the first woman in America to become a millionaire based on her own efforts.

Stephanie Kwolek invented Kevlar while working at DuPont as a research chemist. There was concern that there might be a shortage of petroleum products, so she started trying to develop a fiber to reinforce tires. Why was that important? If the tires were lighter, less gasoline would be needed to propel the vehicle. After a great deal of effort, it was brought to the market in 1971, and it is in everything from skis to shoes to race cars.

The movie *Joy* starring Jennifer Lawrence is loosely based on the wonderful inventiveness of Joy Mangano. Ms. Lawrence brings to life the breadth of this woman's journey and her invention of a self-wringing mop. She went on to invent a whole slew of other household products. The movie, unlike the list of women above whose lives we know little of, laid bare the struggles she had to endure. One of the most painful parts of the movie for me, as I sat in the dark theater, was listening to Robert DeNiro in the role of the father as he cut down his daughter. He said he shouldn't have expected so much of just a housewife. It was brutal. The redeeming family member was the grandmother, Mimi, who kept telling her granddaughter that she could and would be a success. I rooted for Mimi all the way through. Joy needed someone and she was lucky to have a strong woman who loved her enough to encourage her to reach for her dreams.

Spanx are a great invention, as I can personally attest. This invention by Sara Blakely has made her a billionaire, and the product is enormously useful. She undoubtedly had to learn chemistry, business organization, and how to build from the ground up, along with inventory control and retail management. She followed her creative star.

While Misty Copeland is not a scientist, the barriers she broke to be named principal dancer at the American Ballet Theater were many. She is the kind of role model we want: smart, focused, persistent, hardworking, and with a good media presence. Today she is an inspiring example to all women—if you want something badly enough, yes, you can get it.

Put on Your Boots and
Will What You Want

So let's make up our collective minds that we aren't going to sit here and be silent any more. We are going to grab our share of the spotlight, because we deserve it and because we are here and present and ready to be counted. I have willed myself into overcoming fear. I have willed myself into taking a very active hand in deciding my destiny, not the destinies others wanted me to take. Leaving politics was a very affirmative step for me, and it felt right. Now I am willing myself into advocating for women in a broader and more focused way. I'm hoping this effort will benefit my granddaughter and other girls too.

With our Herdacity project, we hope to engage women in a conversation about themselves and what they want to achieve, and to help them reach some successful conclusions for themselves.

For this to be effective, first we have to know who we are. That means our strengths and weaknesses, our likes and dislikes; we need to better understand where we need more courage or more understanding.

Second, I think it is important, each and every day, to choose to be happy. I mean really positive and optimistic. I suspect there is research that says pessimists can do great things, and surely they can; but if I don't see some happiness every day, it is hard for me to move forward. This is not the same as confronting fear. I have a little blue sticky on my computer monitor with the words "choose happiness" and "no negative cha-cha."

When I think about the personal struggles some of my friends and relatives face, I am reminded again of how much I have to be grateful for. So I urge you to make your own list of the reasons you have to be happy. This is more than a standard Thanksgiving list, since it bears repeating daily. Sort of like an emotional vitamin, giving you an extra boost.

Third, find out what you are afraid of, and deal with it in a sensible yet very straightforward way. I love lists so I always gravitate to a list of the problems facing me that seem to make me anxious. And of course, if you are lying in bed stewing about it, get up, drink some water, turn on the lights, and the ringtail in the attic will retreat.

Next, and sometimes at the top of my list, find ways to laugh, and do it often. Get a box with index cards and write down what you did in the preceding week to make you laugh. I love listening to Sirius XM Radio, particularly Laugh USA. I listen to it at least three or four times a week and I do laugh—hard—and it brightens my day. Then look back over the cards and remember the good times. I also love to laugh with close friends. It isn't just the sound of the laugh, it is the knowledge that I am really communicating with someone I care about and the feeling is mutual.

Learn to love something about yourself. On other cards, write down one thing you like about your body. Only pick one. That is all you need. Hair, eyes, skin, hands, feet. There will be something you like. And remember it. There is something in each of us to love.

Have a spiritual center of your own. In my own case, I have a small cross I was given years ago and I leave it in whatever purse I am using. It shuffles around from purse to purse, and when I come across it every day or so, it serves as an unexpected reminder to do good, pursue selflessness, and look for something bigger than myself. Whatever your spiritual center is, use it to help you.

In your daily world, pick something you like to look at or think about each day that isn't related to you but to the world around you. For me it is wind in the leaves, clouds scudding across the sky, or the pinks and reds of sunrise and sunset. As I've said, I also like the sounds of water dripping into a trough or tank. It means we have enough water, and that means security.

Find the rocket fuel of your life that you are going to use as you decide your destiny. Every one of us has something we feel passionately about. That passion creates its own energy, which then enables us to engage in whatever we care about. Don't settle for apathy. Instead— feed the passion. The energy you create will be exciting and it is a powerful boost to those around you. They can feel the energy and it elevates their spirits, giving them a bit of that excitement as well.

In January of 1999, Governor George W. Bush swore me in as Agriculture Commissioner for the State of Texas. He said, "Susan Combs is a woman of high energy. She even makes coffee nervous." It brought down the house. I've always been energetic. I'm not talking about a coffee kind of energy, but one where your zeal and drive to do that one special thing is enough to keep you going. A purpose-driven life is, at least for me, the best way to operate. Being fueled by the drive to do something I love is a powerful motivator.

Find something in your home, apartment, car, or wherever that gives you pleasure to look at. A smooth stone, polished wood, soft fabric, the fur of your cat or dog. A photo of a family member. A present from a much-loved friend. There is something in your life that makes you mentally smile—for even just a second.

Engage your creative side. Can you say something that is interesting and different, or write about it? Or sketch something. Perhaps you are a great whistler. My father was; he truly loved to whistle and it made him so happy to whistle along with music. How about making music yourself? I sing in the car but only with the windows shut. I am not a complete idiot. I also like to dance in the living room and sometimes I sing along there, too. It is hugely liberating and I feel untethered—like the lightest balloon. Look at colors, walk barefoot, feel textures and materials with your skin—feet, hands, arms.

Be sure you have someone or something to love. I am so lucky to love my husband, my three sons and their spouses, and my three grandchildren. Talking to them and hearing about them fills me with real warmth and love. The memories I have of my boys going back decades are legion and, except for the occasional toddler tantrum now in the dim mists of time, they are all good. And I love, but differently, our cat and dog. Our golden retriever just makes me smile, and looking into her eyes makes me aware of how much responsibility I have to her, a helpless animal. We have the wonderful burden of being responsible to those we love and it both enriches and sustains us. I still get wobbly kneed when I think about my sons' arms around my neck when they were babies. Huge melting time. And that is good for us; it fills and nourishes us.

It is also important for us to love outside of ourselves. Do try to love lovable people. I know women who picked very unlovable men and it took years for them to realize their self-worth didn't depend on the men; it depended on their own self, which is why it is called self-worth. My advice is to love responsibly, because you will have responsibility for that person or pet. I obviously didn't love responsibly with my first husband, and that was a hard lesson. But when you value yourself, when you know your own worth, you will not settle for anything less than the best. That, truly, is loving responsibly—you are loving yourself and therefore loving the right person.

Now let's discuss age. The three-letter word that throws fear into our hearts. Well, get over it. In 2016 we had, in the last few weeks of the primaries, three people duking it out for slots on the presidential calendar—one aged sixty-eight, one sixty-nine, and one seventy-four. Their energy levels would match and surpass probably sixty percent of the population. They are not TDO—too damned old, as I call it. So age isn't a limiter. How about the other end of the age continuum? Lots of twenty-year-olds have invented, done start-ups, captured the public gaze. They're not TDY.

Every day, every age is the right day and
the right age to direct our destiny.

So take those old-fashioned lenses off. As long as you have energy, passion, and drive, it doesn't matter if you are the nineteen-year-old lifting the car, or the octogenarian running his kazillionth marathon. Nothing limits you but yourself. Say that again. Nothing limits you but yourself.

Every day, every age is the right day and the right age to direct our destiny.

And yes, get your boots on. Nancy Sinatra's song from 1966 soared to the top of the charts. "These Boots Are Made for Walking . . . all over you." She was referring to a faithless boyfriend, but the affirmation of her strength and a great rhythm made you want to sing and dance along with her. And probably pump your fist as well. She was saying we aren't helpless; we can make things happen. I can move forward, leaving this bad situation behind. We can move to a better place and a better destiny.

Meanwhile, of course, learn to listen for that small voice giving you some insight, that knock on a door to a new life, a new dream. When you hear it, realize you can tackle that new task, one small bite at a time. I have to add that while you are listening to that knock on the opportunity door, make sure to shut out the distractions of people that may not want you to take that path. Be linear, be thoughtful, and you will be able to will yourself into what you want.

To wrap all of this up, my own counsel is to be positive, love yourself and others, and be both patient and persistent in achieving your goals. Whatever those are, those are yours, and they will suit you. No one else can determine who you are. Only you. And, of course, you are exactly the right person to determine your life.

I don't know what I will be doing in five years, but I hope to have laughed a lot, cried only a little, and given and received love. That will make everything worthwhile.

Reading Group Guide

1. Discuss what tenacity means to you in terms of your identity and your pursuits in life. When have you felt good about being tenacious? What allowed you to hold on? When have you felt bad about not being tenacious? What made you give up if you did?

2. Susan had a unique childhood and upbringing, which influenced who she has become. Discuss how you think we acquire our sense of identity. Discuss a time when you preserved a strong grasp on your identity under tough circumstances. What do you think is the most important quality a girl or woman can have when it comes to knowing who she is, being who she is, and holding on to who she is?

3. Discuss the quality Susan possesses that gives her the strength to change course when she has needed to at different points in her life. Discuss why it is important to be able to change. Discuss people you know who are able to change and those who are not, and how their lives have been affected.

4. Susan states that an innate sense of optimism and the wisdom taught to her by her father were key factors in making her the person she is. Discuss why you think optimism is crucial in enabling a person to be successful or a time when it helped you.

5. Susan stresses how important it is for women to defend who they are. Discuss a time when you allowed another person or society to take away a little of your identity or caused you to make a poor decision. Discuss what happens when we don't listen to the voice we have within us. Discuss ways in which you think we can help girls find and hold on to their voice.

6. When Susan's first husband became violent, Susan had friends and a place to go. Discuss how her life might have turned out without that support. Discuss what we can learn from Susan's example about the importance of women having somewhere they can go when they are in trouble. Discuss a time when you needed to leave and did; when you needed to leave and couldn't.

7. Discuss the concept of tenacity as it applies to women and whether it applies differently to men and women. Reshma Saujani, founder of the non-profit Girls Who Code says, "We're raising our girls to be perfect, and we're raising our boys to be brave." She says boys are encouraged to play hard, fall down, get up, and keep going, while girls are raised to be perfect. Trying to be perfect may mean girls give up on themselves if they face a problem they can't immediately solve. Discuss a time when you gave up on something because you thought you would fail before you even began. Discuss why you think this happened.

8. Women and girls are often told, "Calm down." Discuss how and why being "pissed off," as Susan calls it, can be a good thing. Discuss situations where being "pissed off" was motivational and the key to accomplishing a goal.

9. Susan was born into a good family with education and means, and she benefitted from that. But plenty of people with means do not go on to make a difference in their world. Discuss what qualities you think were most important in helping Susan to accomplish all that she has. Discuss what we can do to support success in woman and girls and make sure that success is defined on their own terms.

10. Discuss what you took away from Susan's story about the ringtail cat and the "noises at night." Discuss a time when you overcame fear or specific fears you would like to overcome.

11. Susan shares many scenarios about not fitting in. Discuss how being unusually tall for a woman of her generation may have given her the strength to fight for herself and her causes. Discuss a time or times when you felt you were an outsider and if you think it's likely that everyone has felt this way at some time or another. Discuss an experience in your life in which it was difficult to be different, but one that ultimately helped you survive in another situation.

12. Susan's English roommate from New York City is still a close friend. Friendships tell us something about ourselves and help us bring out parts of ourselves. Discuss why having carefully chosen female friends you can trust is especially important for preserving our identities and pursuing goals in life.

13. Discuss the epigraph of the book that says, "Throw me to the wolves, and I'll return leading the pack." Why do you think Susan selected this epigraph? Discuss times in history or in your life

where a woman or women have been thrown to the wolves as a group or individually. Discuss whether or when they have been able to triumph over this adversity, never mind if they lead the pack. Discuss how this epigraph relates to Susan's life. Discuss how it relates to yours. Discuss how girls can be taught to resist the obstacles in their way and come out victorious.

14. *Texas Tenacity* is full of humor and full of Susan laughing at herself and allowing the readers to do the same. Discuss how being able to laugh at ourselves is important in the struggle for preserving our identities and moving on to bigger things.

15. Susan stresses the importance of finding a cause bigger than we are. Discuss examples of when working for a cause bigger than yourself has illuminated strengths you didn't know you had. Discuss how the things Susan has accomplished, overcome, and fought for have given you insights for how to live your own life.

16. This book is Susan's call to women to direct their destinies. Discuss what in her call appealed most to you. Discuss which one of her stories moved you the most and why. Discuss a situation that Susan experienced that you can especially relate to. Discuss how reading her book has given you the confidence to try something you might not have tried or has changed your opinion on how to pursue a dream that you have had.

About the Author

SUSAN COMBS has spent her adult life blazing trails previously little traveled by women. With a matter-of-fact nature shaped by time on her family's Texas ranch, Susan tackled her years at the all-female Vassar College in a decidedly straightforward fashion. Upon graduation, she worked successfully in high-pressure environments in New York—specifically in international advertising on Wall Street and for a large federal agency. In time, she followed her heart back to Texas and law school and then embarked on a career as a prosecutor focused on securing justice for victims of child abuse.

At a friend's urging, she ran for and won a seat in the Texas House of Representatives where she continued her advocacy for Texas children, mastered the budget process, and pursued efforts to hold government accountable. She was also running a cow-calf operation on her family's century-old ranch in the Big Bend at the same time. Heeding the call to higher office, she was elected the first woman Agriculture Commissioner in Texas history and won praise for her efforts to improve nutrition for Texas schoolchildren while expanding Texas farmers' and ranchers' access to markets through an innovative marketing campaign. She was then elected State Comptroller, where she applied her focus to keep Texas finances in line, as she meticulously collected taxes and paid bills. She advocated tirelessly for greater transparency to ensure the most honest government possible for her fellow Texans.

Since leaving elected office, Susan has been working on Herdacity, an online empowerment community for women, designed to help them stay connected as they blaze their own trails in business, at home, and in the fields of their choosing.